D1085089

508.3152
Blin   Blincoe, Edith.
              Nature walks with
            Edith Blincoe
                    955360

DATE DUE

JUN 3 0 1995			

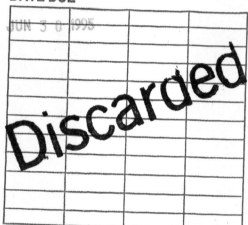

(608) 674-2531

1. Books may be kept two weeks and may be renewed once for the same period, except 7 day books and magazines.

2. A fine is charged for each day a book is not returned according to the above rule. No book will be issued to any person incurring such a fine until it has been paid.

3. All injuries to books beyond reasonable wear and all losses shall be made good to the satisfaction of the Librarian.

4. Each borrower is held responsible for all books charged on his card and for all fines accruing on the same.

DEMCO

NATURE WALKS
with
EDITH BLINCOE

A collection of her columns
from
The Journal Herald

Illustrated by Frank Pauer

955360

ISBN: 0-938492-02-0
Copyright, 1981, The Journal Herald, Dayton, Ohio
Library of Congress Card Catalogue No: 81-83777

To the memory of Ben,
the Senior Ornithologist,
with whom "I walked up the river
and o'er the lea"

Introduction

This book is a product that truly was created, as they say in advertising, because of "popular demand."

The Journal Herald kept getting letters from readers urging us to publish a book of Edith Blincoe's best columns. After several dozens of these missives, we began asking ourselves, "Why not?"

Then some folks from the Dayton Museum of Natural History came to visit, making the same pitch: "We want an Edith Blincoe book." That convinced us.

Edith has been writing for *The Journal Herald* for almost 40 years, and her graceful prose has delighted nature lovers throughout the Miami Valley. Most of the columns in this book, however, are from more recent years. She says her writing has improved since she began in 1942, and she wants to give readers of this book her best.

So here is *Nature Walks with Edith Blincoe*, a compendium of Edith's favorite columns. We hope you like it.

Bill Worth
Managing Editor
The Journal Herald

Foreword

Edith Blincoe's love and understanding of nature had to have come into being simultaneously with Edith Blincoe. She had the advantage of growing up close to nature's world — a circumstance that is rarely possible today. Her training was fundamental and enhanced the learnings that came naturally with non-urban living.

Unquestionably her greatest qualification as a nature writer grew out of the continuing exposure to natural subjects that took place as she trekked woods and fields for many years with her beloved Ben. Her experiences amounted to a never-ending dialogue as she walked fields, observed nesting birds, followed butterflies, pondered mysteries, heard explanations offered, and saw the wonder of the seasons unfold before her. In the process she developed a reverence for nature that approaches her love of God.

One with such a background can be expected to want to share convictions about life's importance with others. So it is not surprising that Edith became a teacher. She spent many years in the public schools where she shared her most precious secrets of nature to inspire her students to learn.

Then she came to the Dayton Museum of Natural History as a volunteer and later as its Curator of Children's Work. There will never be a way that we can measure the effect of this work in bringing the present museum into reality, but, as its director, I can say it was monumental. Her methods became a part of several university courses for teachers of the young. Even today, her courses and concepts are an integral component of the educational structure of the museum.

Intermingled with the other facets of her life, her columns about nature emerged in *The Journal Herald.* Their effect on readers and their understanding of our world is undoubtedly Edith's greatest monument.

"Edith Blincoe says" has become an opening phrase of authority for comments in interchanges concerning the natural happenings in our everyday living.

Her columns are not limited to nature subjects alone. Special features at Christmas, Easter and some other times attract new readers who then follow her to her weekly stories.

Her column following Ben's death has to be read to be shared. Appropriately it serves as the closing column in this book.

We are fortunate to have this collection of Edith's writings, compiled from her columns during her tenure as a naturalist, educator and, most importantly, as a harbinger of nature's eloquence.

E. J. Koestner
Director
Dayton Museum of Natural History

Acknowledgments

To those kind people who wrote to *The Journal Herald* urging the compiling and publishing of these columns in book form, I am deeply indebted. Some I have known, many I have never met, but their interest and effort have warmed my heart.

I acknowledge my gratitude to *The Journal Herald* for making this book possible. It is gratifying, indeed, that the long years of happy association with my paper should produce such a beautiful and lasting record of the column. I couldn't be more pleased.

Certainly special recognition goes to Arnold Rosenfeld, executive editor, and to William Worth, managing editor, who endorsed the publication so agreeably, and to

Virginia Hunt, who with patience and know-how put it all together, and to

Frank Pauer, artist, who made it beautiful with his sensitive art work, the lovely cover and the delightful pen and ink sketches, and to

E. J. Koestner, director of the Dayton Museum of Natural History, for his comments and assistance.

My sincere thanks go to Hannah Coppleston for helping in material selection. Special thanks are due Betty Berry for her aid in organizing material and her never-failing encouragement.

No small acknowledgement of gratitude goes to my son, Joe, who, for the past few years, has faithfully seen that I met my weekly deadline.

Edith Blincoe

Spring

APRIL

Maiden, thy cheeks are wet
And ruefully, thy eyebrows arch:
Is't, as they say, thou thinkest yet
Of that inconstant madcap March?

Robert Loveman

All's well

The year's at the spring:
And the day's at the morn;
Morning's at seven;
The hillside's dew-pearled;
The lark's on the wing;
The snail's on the thorn;
God's in his heaven,
All's well with the world.

I first read this delightful little poem when I was in the third grade. I had no idea what it meant, for our teacher did not discuss it with us. We read it and then copied it in a notebook in cursive writing.

"The year's at the spring." The only spring I knew ran through the milk house on my grandmother's place and kept her milk, cream and table leftovers cool and fresh. *"The day's at the morn"* was meaningless but *"Morning's at seven"* made sense — I always got up at seven.

"The hillside's dew-pearled" simply wasn't true. The dew in the grass sparkled like diamonds and the only pearls I knew, the tiny ones around grandma's pretty cameo pin, didn't shine at all. I knew about the lark being on the wing. There were many larks in the big field beside our house and they flew about and sang as if they were wound up.

I had never seen a snail and the only thorns I knew anything about were the tiny ones on the cabbage rose bush in our yard and they weren't big enough to hold up a ladybug. *"God's in his heaven"* was all right, for where else would He be?

Everybody knew that all was not well with the world. People were all stirred up over the death of a neighbor who was killed by lightning when he sat under a tree during a storm. "Why does God allow such awful things to happen?" I heard grown-ups all around me asking.

I had to grow a lot in understanding before I fully comprehended the meaning of the little spring song Pippa sang as she passed by on her way to work in the mill.

The year's at the spring! Spring has a thousand secrets. They are locked within the seed, the bud, the egg and the wild mother.

The seed never forgets what it is. A violet is always a violet and never does its seed produce the spathe of the coarse skunk cabbage. The bud forever feels the driving purpose behind its function: it always puts forth a leaf or a blossom.

The egg never becomes confused. The robin egg always brings forth a robin and the egg of the spring peeper always produces the tiny frog whose voice hits a note above high C and makes a worthy contribution to the mighty spring chorus.

The wise wild mammal mother knows the secret of the right time to mate so that her young will be born when conditions in the outdoors will provide adequate food and shelter to bring them safely to maturity.

Yet when redbud blushes on April's greening slopes, the first shy violet lifts its sweet face from the brown leaf mold, the robin pulls an earthworm from the moist soil, the wee frog out in the wet field pierces our eardrums with his singing, and a shaky baby rabbit limps across the lawn, spring's secrets have been revealed, even though we do not have the answer to how or why.

(Suggested, in part, by an excerpt from Sterling North's *Welcome, Spring.*)

S P R

The humble bulb

There is nothing in nature more paradoxical than a flower bulb. Most bulbs are ugly, dull-colored brownish gray, lumpish in shape, scabrous and apparently lifeless.

Bulbs are usually rounded but one small bulb I plant in the rock garden and at the edge of the wildflower plot looks like a small cinder lately ejected from a volcanic eruption. I never know which is the business end of the queer looking thing and plant it on faith, hoping it will eventually

reach the light of Ohio skies. Somewhere in the course of its floral evolution it was given the impossible name *chionodoxa.* Mercifully it has a common name, glory of the snow, since it often blooms before the snows of winter melt in advance of spring.

The only bulb I've handled that is attractive and pleasant to the touch is the tulip bulb. It is a lively brown, smooth in texture and looks somewhat like a chestnut. Seeing a bin of them in a nursery center makes one think they look good enough to eat. Then you immediately recall that there have been times in the history of this particular spring bulb when the people of Holland, faced with the threat of starvation, were forced to eat tulip bulbs in order to survive.

A bulb is the last thing in the world you'd select for its beauty and therein lies the paradox, for within the bulb lies the potential of the unique and absorbing beauty found in the floral world. That an inert, unattractive bulb can produce the fragile grace of the lily-of-the-valley, the trilliums, the scillas and squills, jonquils, narcissus and daffodils seems incredible.

Perhaps it is not by chance that these tenderly lovely flowers appear in spring as part of the renaissance of life in our physical world. They are typical of resurrection, glowing, exquisite in form and coloring, delicate in fragrance, the antithesis of their lowly origin, the nondescript bulb.

Walk in your garden and behold the fresh green up-thrusting spears of hyacinth, tulip, crocus, daffodil, squill and behold a miracle. Modern man scoffs at miracles, yet takes for granted or does not notice those that reveal themselves at his feet. For the ugly bulb transformed into the dainty bell of the daffodil, a bed of tulips swaying in a breeze, is a recurring miracle that cannot be explained to the cynic but is reverently enjoyed by the believer and the innocent in heart.

Cedar Waxwings

Cedar waxwings are dropping down in trees throughout the Miami Valley like manna from heaven. A fine flock flew in for a visit in the old apple tree in my garden recently and people have reported seeing small to large flocks in every direction of the compass: from city and rural gardens, from trees along the Stillwater and from park areas.

The sight of these flocks is exciting, not only for their numbers, always a cause for quick attention, but for the effect their silhouettes make against the winter sky: erect, slim, elegant in proportion and posture, topped by a pretty rise of feathers into a neat, precise crest.

Glimpsed through binoculars or seen close-up they have a subtle beauty unlike that seen in any other bird. The blend of brown, gray and yellow on the head and back is soft and subdued, the breast is a delicate shading of saffron that fades to near white toward the tail. Tail feathers are tipped with yellow, making a narrow band of color across the straight tail. A narrow black band extends from the beak and forms a narrowing eyeline that curves upward around the crest. The chin is black and a small placement of white under the eye gives the bird a smart air of chic.

The tip of each wing feather is decorated with a bright red wax-like appendage which seems to add to the length of the shaft. It is believed that these blobs of wax (which incidentally give the bird its

common name) preserve the feathers while the bird flutters its wings to keep balanced as it feeds on berries on many species of fruit-bearing trees. Feathers that lack this wax protection become ragged, so the waxwing's special beauty mark also serves him in a very practical way.

This exotic bird has no song but utters a

"hiss-s-s" that is heard in flight and when it is perched.

Cedar waxwings are mysterious birds, not "spooky" mysterious, but mysterious in the way that many manifestations cannot be explained. For instance, who can answer some of the questions that arise concerning this bird?

Why do they suddenly appear at any time of year, on the hottest day of August or the coldest day of January?

Why are there long time lapses when they are not seen?

Why do they not follow a conventional migration route?

Why do they always travel in flocks?

Being social birds, why don't they nest in colonies?

A prominent ornithologist once wrote this of the cedar waxwing; "He is the perfect gentleman of the bird world.

"There is in him a refinement of deportment and dress; his voice is gentle and subdued; he is quiet and dignified in manner but is never quarrelsome and in his habit of sharing food with his companions, we may read . . . the quality of his politeness, almost unselfishness very rare, almost unheard of in the animal kingdom."

This habit of sharing food is one of the most endearing traits of these birds. The Senior Ornithologist and I once observed probably 10 waxwings on a bough of our old apple tree when it was in full bloom. One bird passed a petal to the one next to

him all down the line, the last bird starting it back on its return journey. At last the petal became so limp a bird ate it, the polite play was over and they all flew off.

I saw my first cedar waxwings many years ago when the S.O. and I were tramping through Forest Park, only a memory now since its site is covered by commercial buildings and blacktop, our present society's symbol of progress. A shallow, but sparkling clear little brook trickled through the lower part of the park and here we found several waxwings sporting in the water, drinking, dipping, shaking their feathers and sending the water into cascades of finest spray. They then flew into the hackberry tree above them where they fed, often returning to the water to drink.

Besides eating fruit, waxwings are highly insectivorous. One May the S.O. found hundreds of this species scattered along the Stillwater feeding on canker worms that infest the hackberry and elm trees.

We also see waxwings feed like flycatchers. They fly from a perch to catch flying insects and return to their perches to eat them. We've seen huge flocks fly out over large inland lakes and feed on aerial insects much as swallows and swifts do.

Somehow, somewhere, the flocks break up to nest singly in a sunny, open thicket or young orchard. The only nest I ever saw was in a young peach tree in the backyard of a home in Englewood.

I   N   G

The earth renewed

If earth had not endured the throes of winter, spring would not be considered a time of resurrection. In one of his short essays, Hal Borland suggests that the new year should start on March 24, the time of the spring equinox, when all life starts anew in the natural world.

Spring can well be called the beginning. The biblical story of the earth's beginning in Genesis is one of great literary richness, its dignity and simplicity unsurpassed.

The only conflict between it and "the theory of evolution," so disturbing to many sincerely devout people, lies in the understanding of time. In the reckoning of time, how long was the biblical day in comparison to the modern 24-hour period of time? A million years? A billion?

Evolution is the great creator at work. It expands and explains the simplistic biblical account of creation. The complex, intricate yet delicate, balance in nature and the interdependence of all forms of life found on our planet that provides the right ecological needs for their survival are so vast and all-encompassing they stun man's finite comprehension.

It was carried into effect slowly — ah, so slowly. How much more meaningful is this slow progressive creation than if it had been accomplished instantaneously as if by the snap of a magician's fingers. We can only look on it with awe and reverence and sing in our hearts, *"My God, how great Thou art."*

Perhaps our conception of the world's creation can be grasped easily when we behold the lofty snow-crowned mountain and the far-flung waters of the restless sea, or hear the rolling thunder after the lightning's flash.

Magnitude and grandeur are synonymous in the human concept of the creator's almighty power. But study the exquisite perfection of the tiny harbinger of spring, a wildflower now blooming in the brown leaf mold of the forest floor. Examine its dainty minute florets, the precision of its small deeply cut leaves. Here we see an entirely different type of creativity from the handiwork of a gentle, compassionate God.

Our present spring stands on the sidelines making a reluctant entrance on nature's stage. Spring needs the quickening effect of sunshine and moisture to hasten maturity in plant life. No matter how late the season is, however, it goes about its appointed tasks.

Weather conditions might vary the norms regarding the appearance of the first wildflower, the first returning robin, the first piercing notes of the spring peeper out in the wet field, but always they are eventually seen and heard.

How very well-behaved our present March has been, a consistent holding back on warmth, with only one day warm without wind, no storms, no quick change from one extreme of weather to another.

Somehow we take everything March brings philosophically. It can have its temper tantrums, it can behave like a charming child or it can rant like a bully and we excuse all its eccentricities because we expect it to behave so. But March's unpredictability gives us physical jolts, stirs us to activity and stimulates our imagination.

March, we need you.

S   P   R

March wind

A wag once said that March can produce 17 kinds of weather in 15 minutes. Perhaps that is a numerical exaggeration, but March certainly is lively. March is a prankster, March is a hardy extrovert. March is lowbrow, rough, earthy. March thrives on variety. March smiles one minute, frowns the next. There is never a dull moment throughout the entire month.

From the earth underfoot to the arch of the sky overhead, March keeps everything stirred up. One day you walk across the lawn. It is sodden underfoot. The Lab gallops off, her huge paws leaving deep tracks in the soft ground, the sere grass flying in uprooted tufts in every direction. A day later you cover the same route and find the ground frozen, so rough and irregular it hurts your feet through the soles of your shoes.

You look out the window and see a brisk snow shower that quickly whitens the grass, decorates the bare branches of tree and shrub, and hides, in a sudden gust of wind, the fallen leaves and mulch on the flower beds. In a swift change of pace March accelerates the wind, sends the laden clouds scooting and soon dissipates the snow when the revealed sun beams his warmth on the land.

March often weeps petulantly and cares not a whit if the drops fall gently to earth or as hail or sleet in a bitter wind.

March smiles encouragingly and in so doing opens wide the buds of golden winter aconite, lifts the drooping head of snowdrop, out in the wet fields and swampland, expands the spathes of skunk cabbage and starts the growth of its broad, coarse leaves.

March's sunlight is eccentric. What a time for a walk, you think, and out you start. But despite the brilliant sun, the air is chilly and you return quickly inside for a coat.

March's idiosyncrasies are revealed in its wind. It is seldom warm. It is often mean, tugging at your clothing, blowing your hair, your whole body struggling with its power, its pull and tug.

March is never relaxed or serene. It is like a finical housekeeper, constantly on the move with a paint brush in one hand and a dust cloth in another. March uses the wind to do its bidding. It clears the pollution from the sky. It prunes dead or dying limbs from trees. Ends of twigs, weakened by winter's changing temperatures, are snapped off and scattered broadcast across the land. It awakens brooks to start clear and sparkling on their journey to the sea. It prods and bullies winter: "like an army defeated, the snow hath retreated." It is a spur to prick the natural world to new life.

March has not found favor with poets. Perhaps it is too strong, too rambunctious for their refined natures. Perhaps the weather is too inconstant for quiet contemplation. Wordsworth wrote a swinging tribute to March, and children and older persons alike enjoy Stevenson's imagery in his poem, *The Wind*:

I saw you toss the kites on high
And blow the birds about the sky
And all about I heard you pass
Like ladies' skirts across the grass.

Why not read the entire poem before March blows out its bluster and gives way to gentle April?

I   N   G

A twilight bird

The sun had set clear. The rosy-orange afterglow sent a lingering light across the field and emphasized the delicate tracery of the terminal twigs on the row of tall trees along its border. At this time "between the dark and the daylight, when the night is beginning to lower," a group of 36 people stood silent on a wide trail that led from the field to a wet woods.

They listened for a sound, an ancient sound that predated by a millenium the drone of an airplane on its way to Cox airport and the swish of cars crossing Englewood Dam. In the advancing twlight they listened for a bird sound and it came, a harsh nasal "peent," a sound that introduces a strange performance enacted by a strange bird, the woodcock.

Initially, the act this bird dramatizes is a courtship performance staged to win his lady love but it continues after mating, nest making and egg laying. The later display asserts in no uncertain terms that the area is occupied and that no trespassers are permitted.

The "peent" is repeated several times and fluctuates in volume, for the male is "dancing" in a circle and consequently, the sound thrusts in different directions. Powerful flashlights pick up the bird as he struts on the ground in front of us, his long beak pointed downward, his tail raised and spread into a stiff rounded fan, his large eyes catching the gleam of the flashlight.

Suddenly, the bird flies up at an angle, its wings making twittering, musical whistling notes. Some authorities think they are vocal. The bird rises in spirals to a height often 200 or 300 feet in altitude and then the true love song is rendered, a loud, three-syllable song, uttered three times while the bird is circling, then it volplanes to earth. The song is loud, clear, musical and deeply stirring.

The display continues until the afterglow gives way to the enveloping darkness of night. On dark nights, the song is heard from dawn to daybreak and on moonlighted nights the indefatigable bird sings until dawn.

The woodcock is a bird of the twilight. Farther north, particularly in New England, it haunts the boggy thickets where alder and willows grow. In Ohio it is found in wet woods and thickets. We once found a nest in an old orchard not far from the kitchen entrance to the farmhouse.

The courtship display, flight and song of the woodcock remain one of the wild, free, accomplished natural performances left us in a modern civilization of noise, confusion and artificiality.

S   P   R

Skunk cabbage

March brings renewed life to the natural world — the first wildflower, the first bird on an incoming migration, the first venture forth of the chipmunk from his snug burrow, the first honeybee flight from its winter hive.

On a walk through the wet woods at Aullwood, I found the magenta spathe of the skunk cabbage wrinkled with age and the florets on the rounded spadix entirely spent. The leaves that appear after the flowers bloom now are thrusting through the muck of the swampy woods from the base of the waning blossoms. They wait, coiled in a tight, thin roll, to expand in the increased warmth of the sun.

Skunk cabbage covers an extended area in this woods. At maturity the leaves are broad and coarse, but they are a bright, lively green and make an attractive ground cover in the dark woods throughout the summer.

Other places in the valley also have fine displays of these plants — Spring Valley, Cedar Bog and in a sunny opening in the beautiful woods at Stoneybrook Farm near Waynesville. Skunk cabbage grows well anywhere it is wet during the growing season, even in wet glacial meadows high in the mountains. When leaves of this plant are bruised or broken, they give off an offensive odor of skunk, hence the common name.

Certainly, skunk cabbage would not take a prize in a wildflower beauty contest; it is coarse, oversized, thick, colored in the somber tones of decaying vegetation of the swamp. And, like a wayward child, it insists on growing in water where it can keep its feet wet.

The woodcock, the first bird to migrate North, is an avian counterpart of the skunk cabbage, but with one exception: He likes his habitat damp, not wet, and the water must be sweet and clean, never sour or foul.

Woodcocks are short-legged, squat birds about the size of a bobwhite, all over a mottled brown, a color that protects them perfectly in their natural environment, the brown leaves of the forest floor. It looks top-heavy as if it might lose its balance and fall on its long beak. This impression is enhanced by the fact that its tail is short, stiff, broad and rounded.

The large eyes are set far back on the sides of the large head. The woodcock is active at twilight in the semi-darkness of woods and dense thickets, so its sensitive sight is essential. Its plumage is lined and blotched, perfectly camouflaged to blend into the lights and shadows of the surroundings. No other species depends so completely for safety upon its coloration.

The bird might sit on its nest of brown fallen leaves and never be seen. The Senior Ornithologist and I once found an incubating female on a nest at Cedar Bog and I stroked her on her back with a twig without her taking flight.

Woodcock young are precocial; that is, they do not require care in the nest. As soon as their natal down is dry they can run around and fend for themselves even though the old birds are concerned parents. They are so well camouflaged it is almost impossible to find them on the ground.

I   N   G

Eerie fog

A fog is a rain cloud come to earth. It can be a mist rising from the river, white, graceful, moving effortlessly with a breeze, soon to be dissipated by the heat of the sun. Or it can be a total, enveloping cloud of condensed water vapor that covers land, or sea or a metropolis like London. It is ghostly and heavy, but has no weight. Often it is dangerous, causing wrecks at sea and collisions on land, with people, birds and animals losing their way.

Always, fog is mysterious, eerie. It changes familiar outlines to weird shapes and forms. Sometimes it blots out all landmarks, and you feel as if you are the only person in the world, enveloped in an airless nothing so dense that you could cut it with a knife, yet you cannot hold a bit of it in your hand.

Such a fog covered my hilltop one morning last week. Visibility was nil, except for the skeletal top branches of the pig hickory at the foot of the hill. My neighbors' houses were nonexistent. The pretty cup of the Stillwater Valley that snuggles between me and the eastern skyline was swallowed in an enormity of swirling gray mist. I felt its burden of microscopic raindrops on my face, my hair, my clothing.

All sound was muted, unearthly. There must have been a fairly large flock of redwings in the hickory tree, for they were singing, their chorus strained through the sieve of the fog's denseness. It was ventriloquial, as if coming from a great distance, the volume thin, but the quality of the music fell strangely sweet and plaintive.

Song sparrows' tinkling tunes came from three directions. They were fey songsters, struggling to keep their identity intact under incredible conditions. This day they seemed to sing in order to retain their status of living creatures.

I walked very carefully in the direction of the mailbox, bumped into it and left my letters for the mailman. I returned to the house, fog lapping at my heels. Later, the fog lifted. In Maine, fog "burns off," but this Ohio fog had nowhere to go but up, unaided by the heat of the sun that did not shine all day.

Grass everywhere is a sickly yellowish tan, for it had little snow for protective cover this mild winter. Now it is at the lowest ebb of attractiveness. Along with its bilious color, it is also thin and straggly.

But the depressing grass wore a ruby gem, the red breast of the first robin I'd seen in my yard this new year. What a welcome sight! I felt my spirits soar, hope reborn. No wonder the Pilgrims were delighted at their first sight of this bird that reminded them of the pretty little redbreast of their English homes.

I looked out another window that frames the small wildflower garden. A male grackle lifted a brown leaf, hunting food. His neck and shoulders shone with a deep iridescence of dark blue and purple and green, his body gleaming black. He took a few steps — his right wing dropped, and he limped, favoring his right leg.

I looked at him with awe. A miracle of survival he was, for he had nested last summer in one of the spruces in my garden and had limped his way about, caring for his young capably, even though handicapped. He has survived the hazards of migration, a precarious winter and returned by choice to the sanctuary of my yard. As one survivor to another, I saluted him.

S   P   R

Wildflowers

And now comes April!

Doesn't the word April have a pleasant sound? It's easy on the tongue, gives a lilt to sound. It conjures up in the mind nascent greening, freshness, watercress in the cold water of the brook, blue skies that suddenly gray over in a pout and pounce the Earth with a quick shower that refreshes and restores.

Overnight the daffodils grew inches taller and showed plump buds. Bloodroot, violets, Dutchmen's breeches and false anemone bloomed in my small wildflower garden and, across the fence in my neighbor's yard, forsythia in full bloom glistened gold. Dandelions blinked in the lawn. What a fine yellow is each round disk nestling in the grass. Why do we fight it?

The early spring wildflowers overcome vicissitudes and stage an impressive show.

I've often stood in awe of the indomitable stamina and determination to survive that these members of the plant kingdom show. They appear at a time when few flowers bloom in the cultivated garden.

Tiny harbinger of spring, almost lost in the brown leaf mold on the forest floor, the entire plant, not much larger than a half dollar, is one of the earliest to appear. It is a perfect thing with its black-tipped stamens in the wee white flower giving it the colloquial name of "salt and pepper." The leaves are deeply serrate and the effect of exquisite proportion and size is a delight to those who like miniatures.

Skunk cabbage appears mountainous compared to the pygmy size of the salt and pepper but it blooms at the same time out in wet woods or swamp lands standing in full sun.

Hepatica with its fairy pastel shades hugs the wooded slopes and makes magic bloom on huge boulders along swift streams in our state parks. The finest growth of this plant in our valley is found at Glen Helen and John Bryan State Park. The dainty beauty of these flowers seen in great masses here stands as tribute to their hardihood, for "they often bloom with their face to the sun and their back to the snow."

After these first wildlings bloom, spring seems to burst out in glee and suddenly every wooded area that has been left free of man's unwise manipulation is a riot of gentle beauty with flowers dainty in color and size. *Anemone, isopyrum* (false anemone), spring beauty, dogtooth violet, the white, yellow and blue woods violet, wild larkspur, sweet william, the many species of trillium, Dutchmen's breeches, corydalis, squirrel corn, celandine poppy, spider wort, bellwort, and the heavenly blue of mertensia along with the gold of marsh marigold, the buttercups, and golden ragwort.

To see one individual of any of the species mentioned is enough to fill one's sight with awe and heart with wonder. To behold them en masse spreading over the floor of the woods, covering the banks of streams, growing out of crevices in rocks, is enough to overwhelm the senses. They are most fragile, yet they have survived frosts, tornadoes, drought and flood.

Of weakness and of strength,
How little can we tell!
I thought the wildflower's bell,
Beside the great oak's hardihood,
The frailest thing in all the wood;
Yet in the storm the wildflower stood,
It was the oak that fell.

Archibald Rutledge

I   N   G

Brown thrasher

In April, when the orchard trees are frothy bouquets of white and palest pink, and redbud and dogwood climb the ravines and ridges and paint them white and lavender-rose with their beauty, the brown thrasher returns to our valley.

He floods the countryside with his music, for he belongs to the mockingbird group of talented singers and is recognized for his gifted performance.

The brown thrasher is a fine large bird with bright cinnamon brown plumage on head, back and tail. The breast is off-white with lines of brown dots giving a neat tailored effect to the bird's appearance.

The warming sun shines on burgeoning trees and shrubs along country roads, on tangled growth in fence rows, on thickets crowded with hawthorne and on hillsides white with bloom of wild plum and shadbush.

Here, away from the crowded ways of man, the brown thrasher sings. Perched on the tip of some large shrub or young tree, head lifted to the sun and sky, long tail drooping, he spills his paean of praise in an ecstasy of sound.

The loud song poured from the treetop is the first step in the brown thrasher's courtship. Any interested female in the region can hear it clearly and it is a defiant territorial claim that warns any ambitious intruding male that the songster has staked his claim and will tolerate no trespasser.

While the bird's music is important in courtship and territorial establishment, it is significant for the place it commands in the evaluation of bird song. Some authorities consider the brown thrasher's song "a brilliant performance, equalled, if judged solely by its technical skill, by few North American birds and surpassed perhaps by only the mockingbird."

Many human interpretations have been given the thrasher's song but I've always liked and found Mrs. H. P. Cook's version apt and amusing. She likened the song to a one-sided telephone conversation set to music, of course, that goes something like this, "Hello, hello, yes yes, Who is this? Who is this? Well, well, well, I should say, I should say. How's that? How's that? I don't know. I don't know. What did you say? What did you say? Certainly. Certainly. Well, well, well. Not that I know of. Not that I know of. Tomorrow? Tomorrow? I guess so. I guess so. Goodbye. Goodbye."

The singing period of this bird has a brief span. We must enjoy the first days of his rapture, for after mating takes place thrashers are quiet and secretive about the nest.

I have always considered the brown thrasher as a rural bird that seeks thick tangles of honeysuckle or wild rose bushes or dense shrubs for nesting. Gardens around city or suburban houses are too refined for his liking but he might move into a rough unkept garden if he can find one.

S　　　　　　　　　P　　　　　　　　　R

Mockingbird

As hoarfrost coats the winter branch with silver-white ice crystals, so April veils with gossamer green each twig and stem and clothes the woods with their first faint greening. It is subtle, this greening, provocative with a hint of unreality.

It lasts so brief a time, this ephemeral loveliness. When the sun shines full on this initial evidence of an awakening world, we are stirred at its light frailty.

Its most elusive beauty comes on a misty morning with a mere hint of sunlight breaking through low clouds that might bring one of April's quick, sweet rains. It is an enveloping scene of tenderness, innocence, complete absence of all that is ugly or evil.

And thus does April bring green to a winter-drab world. All too soon the blossoms and infant leaves on deciduous trees mature and the illusory veiling becomes a memory, giving way to fully developed foliage that makes canopy for the undercover of the forest floor, a filter for the sun's increasing heat.

Every growing thing seems to be in a hurry. Overnight a wildflower pops up into full bloom without a preparatory hint of its intention. Today it was mertensia, or Virginia bluebell, and the celandine poppy, its round yellow orb a pretty foil for the bluebell's blue.

As I worked in the garden, a cardinal burst into an ecstatic song, but then it sang like a titmouse, followed immediately by the scream of a blue jay, and I realized that I was hearing instead the medley of a talented mockingbird.

I located him in the top of the old maple tree. What a musician! Before he took a breather he had imitated geese, killdeer, titmouse, brown thrasher, cardinal and crow, all intermingled with pretty tunes of his own. I don't remember having heard before such perfect imitations as this bird rendered. Was it his closeness, the beauty of the warm sunny morning, my own receptivity that made his music so special? Or was it the fact that I had not heard the mockingbird sing for several years?

Mockingbirds had been victims of the 1977 hard winter, and their numbers have been sadly depleted. Their increase in population has been slow. At any rate this mocker was quite a virtuoso and I heard him all the time I was out, now close by, now at a distance, singing his heart out in praise of the fine day.

I wish I might have witnessed the interesting bird experience friends enjoyed in their garden the past week. The large magnolia tree in their garden was visited by a flock of 19 cedar waxwings. These dainty birds fed from the open cups of the flowers, probably on small insects attracted to their nectar. But what was most unusual, several nestled down in the flowers, very still, as if taking a nap. There was no fluttering of feathers as if bathing on accumulated moisture in the flower — just a brief period of complete relaxation before flying off.

Being able to observe cedar waxwings close up is always a special joy. They apparently enjoy one another's company, for they are polite and considerate. Seldom do we see an individual bird, for they travel in small to very large flocks. One would think that such a social species would be colonial in nesting, but that is not the case.

My beautiful week of outdoor activity closed on a sad note. Either my resident male cardinal or the rival he had been feuding with for some time was killed by a passing car. At dusk I heard the robin's first complete, full-throated song, a fitting requiem.

Cedar Bog

From time immemorial swamps have been considered places of darkness, mystery, danger and fear. Many were hideouts for outlaws and people escaping from some harsh law or social injustice.

A swamp has an absorbing appeal to the naturalist. It is a place of wonder, a challenge to his stamina and a stimulus to his study of all forms of wildlife in its environment.

Cedar Bog, located between Springfield and Urbana, is within easy reach of local outdoor observers. It is a glacial swamp formed between two widely separated ridges. Originally it was of vast extent, but it gradually filled in. Through its area a small stream, clear and unpolluted, flows. It maintains a constant temperature and the water has been tested and found safe for drinking.

One of the mysteries of the swamp is the gathering of methane gas on the surface of the creek in areas where decaying vegetation has collected.

An extensive boardwalk makes walking in the swamp easy. It also protects the delicate balance of survival of plant life here, for humans' indiscriminate plunging through the black muck is extremely destructive.

Plant life of the bog is luxuriant and varied. The unique feature is the white cedar or alba vitae, a tree of the far north which was brought this far south by the ancient glacier. It is a fine pyramidal tree that reaches a height of 50 feet.

In the deciduous woods the buxom green foliage of skunk cabbage covers the forest floor. Equally widespread and now blooming are trillium grandiflora and the showy marsh marigold.

But there are also, easily identified from the boardwalk, swamp violets, wild lily of the valley, Canada Mayflower, anemone, several species of solomon seal, wild flag (iris), bellwort, Jack-in-the-pulpit, nodding, sessile, and red trilliums, toothwort and ferns.

A strange contradiction is the presence of plants that normally are found in open, sunny, prairie-like conditions. Golden ragwort found usually in the sunny edges of woods and in solid, sometimes poor soil, flourishes in this swamp.

An exciting succession of bloom is found until late fall, in July the beautiful flowers that bloom in the hot sun of the prairie and in September the exquisite queen of all, the fabulous fringed gentian.

S   P   R

Bluebird

Van Dyke thought the bluebird, "shaking the tune from his wings while he is flying" sang, in part:

Blue above, you to love
Purely, purely, purely.

I suppose you can put human words to any bird song. Sometimes they are apt. Sometimes they make no sense at all. I always resented the widely accepted interpretation of the tender, ethereal song of the white-throated sparrow, as "Old Sam Peabody." Sam may have been a local hero or saint, but I've always pictured him as a wrinkled old man, as far removed from the delicate beauty of the white-throat's song as the most distant star.

But by stretching my imagination a little, I concede that the bluebird might come close to saying, "truly, truly" as it flies overhead or comes to rest on the telephone wires along a country road.

It is a gentle, musical note as pleasing as the gentle bird that utters it. Everything about this bird is gentle. The flight through the air or from one perch to another is soft, noiseless, and sweeps along with grace. On back and wings is the softest, most pleasing shade of blue and the muted rosy breast blends so unobtrusively with the blue that the entire picture is one of finished perfection.

This summer I'm drinking to the fullest my enjoyment of this dear bird. I see bluebirds every walk I take and in the evening, when I sit on the long upper veranda of the lodge where I stay, they often come to perch in the dead oak at the corner of the building. I'm on eye level with them and can observe their beauty and gentle behavior closely.

One evening a pair flew in to this tree. Another came, and another until nine bluebirds had arrived. Most of them had the white spotted breasts of the juveniles but the rest of their bodies was covered with the heavenly bluebird blue and they communicated with each other with refined and musical "trulys."

One day I saw the old birds feeding a late brood, and another time a loose flock of 16 individuals flew along a densely grown up fence row, traveling along slowly, singing sweetly, evidently enjoying the company of their kind.

Adams County apparently is the bluebirds' Garden of Eden. Propitious sites for their nesting are found everywhere, but of equal importance, here, they are rid of two of their most pestiferous enemies, the starling and the house wren. I haven't seen either of these species since I've been here.

Which must prove a point. Freed from these two sources of trouble, the resulting healthy population of bluebirds indicates that this bird is capable of doing very well for itself where it does not have to struggle with two aggressive species with which it is physically unequipped to do battle.

I   N   G

Life-producing rain

Rain fell straight down from the leaden sky for almost the entire day. As it soaked into the dry earth it wrought the miracle of spring. Before one's wondering eyes the grass greened. The yellow tips of winter that remained in spots on the lawn disappeared and Ireland itself could not boast a deeper, livelier green.

Those who live close to the earth have felt, from the beginning of man's awakening consciousness, the vast rhythms of earth movements, its change of seasons, daylight and darkness, the summer and winter solstice, phases of the Moon in its relation to night light, the ebb and flow of the oceans' tides.

As his comprehension expanded there came a feeling of kinship with the earth as from it he sought shelter, food and clothing to protect his skin from too much exposure to the sun or the winter's cold.

Modern man struggles to find his place in the universe of which he is so significant a part. But he now accepts smugly, as his right, without understanding or curiosity, the comforts that technology, produced by the inventive genius of a few, provides. Thus he alienates himself from his natural environment.

He looks on rain, that life-producing miracle, as a nuisance rather than a blessing, since it often interferes with some planned pleasure. The only good day is a sunny day. Our weather experts are proponents of this philosophy, apologizing when they forecast rain.

There are many kinds of rain and they largely depend upon the velocity of the wind, not so much on the measure of the waterfall for their distribution.

There is the sudden summer shower, largely local, blown across the heavens by a playful breeze. It falls to earth often when the sun shines. It is quickly spent, but it refreshes the dusty earth and sets the robins singing. Summer showers in hill country form quickly, angrily, from skies gunmetal gray, attended by bombarding thunder and lightning. They soon pass with rumbles of thunder to impress you that they meant business.

Rains that come from cloud cover extending from one horizon to another, with little or no wind, are the life-giving rains that send joy and hope into the life of the countryman. They sink deep into the ground and build the water table against possible drought and assure fine crops and abundant harvests.

There is the raw, chill rain of late autumn, a rain that slants against a complaining wind. It penetrates clothing, drips down one's neck and makes the use of an umbrella meaningless. It is the kind of rain that impelled Paul L. Dunbar to write

*The rain streams down like harpstrings
  from the sky.
The Wind, that age old harpist, sitteth by,
And ever as he sings his low refrain
He plays upon the harpstrings of the rain.*

S   P   R

Respectable sparrows

Ornithologists often list the thrushes as a "family of sweet singers" and so they are. But another group of birds, the sparrows, can make the same claim and give the thrushes stiff competition in the avian music department.

Perhaps no other birds are as misunderstood as sparrows. The word "sparrow" immediately sets up a mental image of the English sparrow, alien, brassy, messy and ever-present nuisance. Unfortunately many people put all sparrows in the same class with this unpopular bird so unwisely introduced to our continent in 1850.

Many of our native sparrows that are entirely respectable, with endearing manners and reputations for having economically beneficial feeding habits, look somewhat like English sparrows. They have the same brown and tan, brown and white streaked plumage, they are comparable in size and they have the same broad, blunt conical bills.

Along with this sedate body coloring, however, native sparrows have other characteristics that aid in identification. For example, the field sparrow's crown is a pretty reddish brown and the bill is pinkish. The chipping sparrow is smaller than most sparrows with an unmarked breast and a jaunty russet-colored crown smartly edged with a white eye-line. The song sparrow's breast is streaked with a pronounced central black spot. All sparrows are trim, neat, well-tailored in appearance.

The sparrow family includes finches, cardinals, grosbeaks, towhees and several allied species like the dickcissel. There are around 250 species and sub-species found in North America.

Sparrows produce some of the most beautiful music to be heard outdoors. Perhaps the white-throated sparrow sings the most exquisite song of any American bird. It is so ethereal, so spiritual that it has a singular emotional effect on those who hear its pure sweet notes. It can never be taken casually. One stops, all other senses suspended, and gives full attention to the heavenly song. Those who interpret its song as saying "Old Sam Peabody, Peabody" are guilty of base desecration.

The fox sparrow, Bachman's sparrow, song sparrow, goldfinch, purple finch and others sing delightful songs. The vesper sparrow and white-crowned sparrows' music is most pleasing when heard close at hand. At a distance it loses volume and sounds somewhat metallic.

The small chipping and grasshopper sparrows and the junco have insect-like songs and while the results are not musical, they do not grate on the ear.

The field sparrow, however, has a lovely song that comes close to the white-throat's in purity and simple beauty. It has a throbbing quality that moves one's spirit. I always like to quote the late Dr. Benedict from the University of Cincinnati, who once said, "In the morning the field sparrow sings of hope, in the evening it is a song of faith."

Spring tree bloom

Two trees, the redbud and the dogwood, complement each other at the time of April's mystic greening. The redbud's rosy-purple flowers bloom before the leaves emerge and appear on the entire tree, from stout branches often to the trunk.

The tree is a mass of bloom, yet the effect is light and airy, for redbud grows much like the apple tree with branches widely spread to the light and forming a flat open crown. Like the apple tree, it does not grow to great size.

Each tiny floret is pea-shaped and placed so artistically the natural grace gives the tree the quality of studied perfection. This week the flowering of the redbud is at its best, and its beauty washes the sunny openings in the woods, on slopes and along banks of streams with a poignant loveliness.

A counterpart of our redbud is found in southern Europe, the Orient and Judea. It was in Judea that the redbud received the common name, Judas tree. The legend sprang up that Judas, after betraying his Lord, in remorse hanged himself in a redbud tree and thereafter it was referred to as the Judas tree.

The tiny floret of the redbud reminded Linnaeus, the famous botanist who classified and named the redbud, of a weaver's shuttle; so he gave it the name Cercis, the Greek word for shuttle. *Cercis Canadensis* is the scientific name that places it as a plant growing in the New World.

The redbud is an ancient tree dating from the Eocene geological period. It has great stamina, and though it is not long-lived it has the ability to renew itself through scattered seeds and new sprouts growing from its roots.

The pure white bracts of dogwood appear when the rosy-purple redbud blooms. Dogwood, like drifting snow, appears in sunny openings in the woods and at the wood's edge. Professor Werthner, in his book *Some American Trees*, considered the dogwood "the pride of American woods."

What a marvelous companion it makes for the rosy-hued redbud growing near; how well each tree shows off its own distinctive charm in the misty green of the April countryside.

Dogwoods do not grow to great size, although they reach old age. The flowers form a tight green cluster, each tiny green floret complete and surrounded by four white bracts often mistaken for petals.

The foliage is a heavily textured green leaf that turns a glowing rosy red in autumn. In spring dogwood is a virginal white; in autumn it burns like forest fire.

All facets of the dogwood's life history bring beauty and unique forms of development. Its flowers produce brilliant red berries that are relished by 42 species of birds. By the time berries flaunt their color, the next year's flower buds are already formed. They appear at the end of a two-pronged stalk, round and flat like thick little buttons.

Some seasons the small tree hangs lush with its finished production, the burning berries of autumn and the assurance of springtime resurrection, when in April the plump little flower buds turn the tree white as new-fallen snow.

S P R

Bee fly

April holds the outdoor enthusiast entranced. In order to weave her spell in our part of the Midwest, April must hold a tight rein.

Temperatures must remain on the cool side; there must be intermittent periods of sunshine and shadow; an assurance of light or no frost, and the sun must moderate its heat. If precipitation maintains a correct balance and a just-right amount of rain falls, there follows a miraculous uncurling of leaves, a blossoming of flowers. The earth is enveloped in a misty, tender emergence of green, the landscape a Carot water color, a will-o-the-wisp of no substance. Lovely, pixie April.

Miracles unfold around us. How aware we must be, how alert, lest we miss a single episode in the burgeoning life about us. It might be helpful, also, to have a 10-year-old grandson whose quick perception and alertness does not miss much, as a companion. I would have walked past the fresh-open daffodil but Joey lifted its long trumpet and found the tiny insect with a long proboscis sipping nectar from the flower.

What a wee piece of perfection this insect was! I'd never seen its kind before and did not know its name. The body was round and covered with yellow fuzz, like a miniature bumble, but it was no bee because it had only one pair of wings.

And what wings they were! Outspread, taut, the upper edge a straight line, almost black and the edging of this dark area was scalloped. The lower part of the wing was translucent and the entire wing was heavily veined. The proboscis was as long as the body.

Of course further exploration was delayed until the little creature was identified. We found its picture, greatly enlarged, in our insect guide — a bee fly! We learned that the bee fly never folds its wings over its body; that it is a swift flier; that it is active only in daylight; that it feeds on nectar; that it rests on the ground or a stone or a twig; that it lays its eggs on the ground near the nests of bees or wasps.

In a very elementary way we learn from April the profound and inexorable lesson of the interdependence of every living form of life. How easily Joey learned that the exciting little fly depended on that flower for food and that the special physical organ the proboscis, that made it possible for it to obtain this necessity for life, compensated for the fly's minute size by being abnormally long.

He learned, also, that this fly was useful, as well as beautiful, cunning and delightful to observe. He learned that the pollen that clung to the fuzzy body of a bee fly was carried to other flowers and fertilized the seed so it could produce another plant.

I could not bring myself to tell the happy questioning child, introduced to a source of interest and beauty of which he had not been previously aware, that the safety of the bee-like fly was precarious, indeed. Especially if it crossed the path of a zealous gardener armed with spray can and bent on eradicating any creature that flies, creeps or crawls over the foliage of her plants, that must, by any means or effort, be kept perfect.

I   N   G

Melodious river

Little rivers are as charming and delightful as well-behaved children. Merrily they run their course, twinkling in the sunlight, dreaming as the moonlight gently touches their waters in the hush of night. The pure melody of little rivers singing as they flow swiftly on their way to the sea mingles with the music of bird song all along their journeying.

Little rivers sing in soprano and alto voices; sopranos, light and airy, carry the tune as the water hurries over gravelly beds. There comes a fall or a tumble of rocks in the way and as the water chortles over and around the obstruction the music deepens into alto tones. Where the force of the rivers flowing has washed out depths for swimming holes or places for fish to spawn, there is silence and repose.

A little river I know flows through a farm I visit occasionally and its Indian name, Tawawa, is as melodious as the music it makes. It flows through some level land, then reaches a hilly section where tiny rapids form and the water runs white with foam. It has twisted around the base of a hill, cut into the bank and formed a deep pool where fish grow fat and lazy.

This lively little river with its winning ways flexes its muscles when it grows robust with winter's melting ice and snow and is swollen with early spring rain. In its show of strength it has undercut the roots of two aged sycamores along its banks and toppled them to the ground. The unrelenting pressure of its flow threatens the large culvert through which it sweeps along to join the Miami.

It rained the day I recently walked along Tawawa's singing waters. The raindrops formed circles that spread and broke. The greening grass and swelling buds on trees, and bird song all around bespoke spring. A kingfisher claims the river as his own and patrols up and down the stream. Robins sing in the rain. A Carolina wren sings frequently. This energetic songster has the artist's flair for variety and timing. His repertoire is not limited to one tune repeated until one grows tired of hearing it. One pretty air follows another, nicely selected and rendered at well considered intervals.

A cardinal carols as if it were a sunny May day and a titmouse is heard up the hill toward the house where it pays frequent visits to the well-stocked feeding station on the long deck outside the sitting room windows. Woodpeckers drum on the trees along the path and a bluejay is a blue streak as he flies from one tree to another.

In the undercover of the woods a flock of juncos fly about flirting their white outer tail feathers, lighting the gloom of the woods.

It's relaxing to walk in a misty rain. Sounds, colors and movement are muted, distances cannot be accurately estimated. It's folly to be hurried. You give yourself up to the pleasure of the moment: the joy of walking with cherished friends, the antics of our hostess' friendly dog who frisks gaily with us along the river and through the woods, and the unpretentious, pastoral beauty all about as we walk in the rain.

S   P   R

Woods walk

The country is a kaleidoscope of changing color, movement and song. Events swiftly flow from one rhythm of pulsating life to another. Before we have thoroughly assimilated the beauty of color and fragrance of one aspect of spring, it is gone, followed, in turn, by another succession that quickly lives out its short existence on Nature's time table.

This swift passing is best illustrated by our native wildflowers. The first wildlings, with a few exceptions, are dainty, fragile, with delicate pastel coloring. The flowers are small and the foliage, fine, serrate, often lacy, is proportionate in size. Already most of their bloom is spent and coarser, more robust flowers are having their day.

On a recent walk through a woods having a dense undercover, I found patches of wild phlox, lavender and rose, making bold patterns of color on the forest floor. Bluish purple stalks of wild larkspur rose darkly from fallen leaves and columbine's drooping heads showed a faint orange. These plants are strong and lack the frailty of earlier bloom.

I came out of this unspoiled woods that the owners leave undisturbed onto a flood plain. It is broad, grass-covered. The Stillwater flowed serenely past, its banks lined by fine old forest trees that showed leaves no larger than squirrels' ears. They waved April's floating green veil as far as I could see down the stream.

In the grass stitchwort grew in masses of white. Stitchwort is a respectable member of the chickweed family that has a bad reputation for being a troublesome weed to farmers and gardeners. Each petal of this pretty flower is deeply cleft. To keep the stitchwort company spring beauty grew abundantly and false anemone, which always grows prolifically in a flooded area, flourished here.

In spring the outdoors observer is particularly sensitive to the relation that exists between plant and animal life. All his senses are attuned to the resurrection of life after the latent resting period of winter. The keen awareness of burgeoning nature stirs the use of sight, sound, smell and touch simultaneously and his sense of feeling is done more with his spirit than with the touch of his fingers.

Unseasonal warm weather caused an early arrival of warblers and we hear their weak voices high in the trees where they feed on tiny caterpillars that have emerged in the unusual heat and are feeding on the tender green leaves. Warblers eat tremendous amounts of food and the value of their feeding is inestimable.

Goldfinches' color change is now complete. They look like some exotic blossoms that have miraculously been given the gift of flight. They do not feed so often at the thistle seed now, but they have not deserted the garden they visited so regularly during winter's lean days. They sing from the old maple, the Norway spruces and the lower level of trees in the wildflower garden, little Tommy Tuckers, singing "thanks" for past suppers.

I   N   G

Chimney swift

April presented May with a parting gift of great price. On the last day of her gentle sway, the happy chitter of the chimney swift announced the busy little bird's return to the skies over our valley.

It's to the skies you must look for this small bird dark gray, almost black, with a body that looks like a comfortable rotund cigar, with hardly any tail, but with long, narrow, slightly angular wings. There's great strength in the wings, for they carry the swift zigzagging through the hours of the day pursuing the aerial insects on which it feeds.

There is nothing commonplace about this bird of the air except perhaps its plumage, gunmetal gray without a single dash of color to relieve its unpretentious lack of beauty.

Here is a bird that flies over our broad land from coast to coast and lives its entire life without alighting in trees or coming to rest on the ground. Its entire life history is different from that of any other species and the way it is physically equipped to live its useful life is a story that demands respect, even awe, from the dominant human.

Before the arrival of settlers to the North American continent, chimney swifts were not abundant. They gathered to roost and nest in large hollow trees or on the walls of caves and canyons. The most prominent part of the structure of the settlers' log cabins was the large, brick-lined chimney. This feature was quickly discovered by the swifts.

Nature developed sharp recurved nails on the toes of the swift and it was no trick for it to use this equipment to cling to the coarse bricks of the chimney to roost. To assure added safety in perching, the short, stiff tail feathers end in a sharply pointed tip that easily penetrates the rough surface of the brick. Thus the swifts are safely positioned for long periods of rest.

At the approach of the breeding season, glands that secrete a gluey saliva start functioning in the mouth. The swift flies over the top of deciduous trees and snaps off a dead twig either with its beak or feet, we are not certain which, and carries it to the chimney where it is glued in place. Soon an attractive, lattice-like nest is completed, shining as if it had been shellacked by an expert.

Often the nest is too fragile to hold the family load and it breaks loose from the chimney wall and falls. The young, not yet ready to fly, cling instinctively to the wall with their tiny toes and immature tails until ready to fly, having been fed capably during the interval by the old birds.

The beak of the swift is small and ineffectual. The mouth is wide, extending from ear to ear. The muscles controlling the mouth are weak and the bird flies with its mouth wide open. Insects fly into the mouth as the swift follows their erratic flight. Swallows and swifts feed in the same manner. It is a pretty sight to follow their food flights in the blue skies of late spring and summer.

Time was when aerial traffic was heavy with the passage of these birds, but the uncontrolled use of poisonous sprays has reduced the supply of mosquito food. Eating poison-infected insects has also killed many of these fantastic birds of the air. We face the ultimate tragedy of empty skies.

S   P   R

Ah! May

May! The ancient Romans named this month for Maia, mother of Mercury. May Day was celebrated in Old England on the first day of the month to welcome spring. May queens and May pole dances waxed merry all over the land. Sadly, this pleasant custom is no longer prevalent, for the last May pole in London was taken down in 1717. May Day is called Mary's Day in the Roman calendar.

May has been beautiful beyond anticipation in the Miami Valley, beyond any criterion of comparison. There was perfect weather, beneficent sunshine and rains when needed. Result? Lush vegetation everywhere: Wildflowers, meadows and woodlands flourished, breathtaking in form and color, exciting in strength, heartwarming in grace and beauty.

Man's labor, reflected in the lacy bloom of orchards, the turnover of rich soil ready for seeding, the Irish green of meadows, causes one to dwell on the ancient dignity of the farmer who husbands the land.

In our English heritage the word merry occurs constantly. It's such a happy word. It suits all sound, movement, activity that motivates each day like the music of a carousel. The merry music of the brook, gurgling, laughing like a happy baby; the merry drone of bees sated with nectar; the ear-splitting song of spring peepers out in wet fields, the titillating of birds madly in love and shouting their joy to the entire world.

At Aullwood the jolly little indigo bunting sings in sunny reaches all along the merry little brook, now swollen to importance by recent rains. It is not in this bird's disposition to take a single event in his life seriously, so he sings the summer away.

This little sparrow is a child of the sun, for without its warm rays he'd have little to sing about. The refraction of the sun's light on his plumage produces his dazzling indigo blue and makes him one of the most colorful sights of the countryside. His jazz song is a happy jangle of notes, quickly performed.

The meadow at Aullwood houses a valuable treasure — a pair of nesting bluebirds with four young. A long list of birds that are admirable parents can be made, but bluebird males merit the top place on the list. Concentrated observation of bluebirds feeding young at the nest demonstrated that parental instincts and a sense of parental responsibility are highly developed in the male bird.

This day as we watched the parent birds coming and going with food for the young, it was apparent that the male bird made more frequent trips than the female.

It would be impossible to evaluate the effect this bird has on people. On almost every field trip, every one wants to see a bluebird; and, when we are fortunate enough to have one fly before us on the trail, the ohs and ahs of delight register their pleasure.

The plumage is an indescribable blue — soft, of lovely texture — and the rosy tan of the breast forms a perfect contrast. The color effect is cool, but not remote, for there is an immediate rapport between the bird and the observer.

A poet once said of its song "it blends in a silver strain, the sound of laughing water, the patter of spring's sweet rain."

Ah, May! Forerunner of June's perfect days. What magic can June produce to surpass or even equal the loveliness of all your days, just past?

I   N   G

Towhee

There is a fragile tenderness, an innocence of form and color, a delicate daintiness about early wildflowers that put them in a class by themselves.

Yet they are tough. Consider how they grow. They come up in the cold, some in a wet cold, some dry. They thrive in the direct, unrestrained light of early spring. Nothing in their environment prevents light from reaching them. There is no shade in forest, swamp or field.

The warmth they receive comes from the sun, just beginning to show increased heat following the vernal equinox. Only in the woods is that heat deflected by the slatting effect of the bare trunks and branches of the trees.

By the time leaves on trees are mature, the early wildflowers are gone. They have thrust their frail beauty in bloom through the leaf mold of the forest, the muck of the swamp, the grass of the fields. They have produced seeds, the ultimate functioning of the plant, in a period of about six weeks. After the middle of May wildflowers are sturdier in structure, more robust in color.

When that three-named member of the sparrow family, the towhee, appears, one of our showiest early wildflowers, the marsh marigold, is at its best.

One of the places to see this fine flower at its best is Cedar Bog. In recent years board walks through the bog make a field trip to this outstanding glacial swamp pure joy. The observer doesn't destroy plant life by trudging through the swamp itself and can be more relaxed in his study when he is free from anticipating tripping on a hidden root and landing on his face in swamp muck.

On a much smaller scale these plants grow in the wet woods and along the wildflower trail at Aullwood.

Marsh marigolds are a bright yellow and the leaves are rounded and a dark waxen green. This wildflower does not have the ethereal frailty of most early wildlings, but its freshness, the special "Easter" yellow of its blossoms, its placement in or near water, relieve it of any coarseness or feeling of "spring is bustin' out all over" heartiness. It is reserved, occupying with calm composure its specified place.

And nearby the towhee sings. He is truly a handsome bird. About robin size, the male is black on head, throat, back and wings. His black tail has white outer feathers and the tips are white, which gives him a chic style as he flits about in the underbrush. His breast is pure white but his sides are deeply washed with robin red, which gives him the second of his three names, ground robin. His mate is good looking, too, but is brown where the male is black.

As he communicates with his mate he utters a strong call — "che-wink" — and consequently he earned the colloquial name, chewink. The music that he performs during the breeding session is sung from the tip of a small tree, the melodious notes of "tow-ah-hee." It has been interpreted as saying, "Drink your tea." The song indicates the name, towhee, the name he bears most commonly.

Towhees scratch on the ground chicken fashion for their food in the undergrowth at the edges of woods, open thickets, perhaps in your home gardens, for they are friendly birds. They nest low in native shrubs or low trees and sometimes on the ground. Wherever they're found they add beauty and charm to sight and sound of burgeoning spring.

Birdsong

This morning I walked out into a sunny May day, crisp and cool, the grass sparkling as if sprinkled with diamonds, the sky blue, blue, blue. What a contrast, what a relief from the sodden, gray, rain-dripping skies of the past weeks.

Every living, growing thing seemed bent on responding to the warmth of the sun. New vitality flowed through water-logged plants, stems of flowers straightened, leaves expanded, flowers brightened and glowed.

Bird song was delirious. Bird music is always at its best the first few days in May. Ornithologists like to give scientific reasons for birds singing: establish territory, attract a mate, etc., but why do we, in order to be scientific, belittle the premise that birds sing for pure joy? I was so glad to see the sun I burst into song myself and there isn't anything scientific about my singing.

Along with all the robins, song sparrows, cardinals, meadowlarks, doves, mockingbirds, Carolina wrens, and titmice singing in a well conducted chorus, a talented songster gave a solo performance. This bird wasn't trying to attract a mate, neither was he interested in staking out a territory. He was just passing through the valley on his way north to his breeding grounds. He chose to rest awhile and luckily for me, as he rested, he burst into this lovely song. Out of my own joy, I sensed the joy in his singing.

This visiting musician was the strikingly beautiful rose-breasted grosbeak. His coat is black and white and his head is glossy black. His snow-white breast has a showy shield of soft rosy red. The ivory colored beak, stout and blunt, is sharply contrasted against his black head.

Of all migrating birds that pass through our area in the spring, perhaps the rose-breasted grosbeak has the most accommodating manners. The bird is never hurried or nervous. Calmly he settles himself on his perch where he sings. No matter how many excited bird watchers gather under the tree to see and hear him, his poise is not shattered. He suffers no stage fright and gives a perfect performance.

It is difficult to describe this grosbeak's song. It is deep, melodious, rich, very much like the robin's song but more continuous without the breaks heard in the robin's roundelay. There are no "squeak-squeaks" at the end like those that keep robin music from being perfect and finished.

My visitor sang continuously for about 4 to 5 minutes, a stirring compliment to the sun's emergence from a long period of gloom.

God's first temples

It seems incredible that the fragile and minute harbinger of spring, one of the first flowers to emerge in the spring from the litter of last year's fallen leaves on the forest floor, is akin to the gigantic oak tree whose gnarled branches spread toward every point of the compass. But related they are, even though they are unlike in looks and size, for both are members of the plant kingdom.

Trees have need of food, water, air, light and warmth; without these they would perish. Like living animals they grow, reproduce, work and rest. How they grow distinguishes them from shrubs, their closest look-alike in the outdoors — trees have a single erect trunk that bears a crown of branches and produces fruit.

But trees are more than their botanical description. The mind boggles at the practical value of a tree. Before man had developed speech, humans had dwelt in trees. Then, in that dim distant time when some human accidentally started a fire, fallen branches from some tree fed the first flame.

The use of trees kept step with man's developing intelligence, providing heat and light in the darkness, fortification for safety and ultimately lumber for dwellings and furnishings. Trees played an important role in the rites of primitive religions. Eventually, lumber by-products became increasingly important and remain so to the present time.

Native fruit and nut trees have always provided important food for man and wildlife. Throughout the years, horticulturalists have added to trees' significant contribution to man's comfort and well-being by improving on native species of trees and producing new species, most showing improvement on original forms.

No monetary value can be placed on the contribution trees have made to man's mental and spiritual health, peace and serenity. His spiritual outreach has often been realized through the blessing of trees in his environment.

The grandeur of trees fills the sensitive person with awe; the size, the towering height, structure and expanse of crown against the calm summer sky or the storm's wild blast, show up the human and reduce him to size. Their grandeur is comparable to

S   P   R

the solidity, the never-changing steadfastness of the eternal hills.

I shall always remember some large trees that have filled me with a feeling of humility and reverence, one a mighty maple tree in the yard of a farmhouse in Adams County. Its shade covers a large, two-story dwelling and part of a wide expanse of lawn.

An enormous sycamore at Aullwood is a compelling sight; the white bark against the blue sky scintillates. Often in May I've seen my first Baltimore oriole high on its outer twigs, its vivid coloring radiant in the sunlight. This bird often swings its hanging nest in the tree, and the warbling vireo sings from its branches overhanging the brook that keeps the sycamore's feet wet.

Then there are the ancient beech trees in the woods on the Bradley Schaeffer farm. The beautiful, smooth, gray bark is unblemished by carving; the geometrical placement of branches perfect, the entire beech grove within the woods unscathed by time, passing storms or depredation by man.

Montgomery County Parks have spectacular examples of oak trees in the fabulous "Three Sisters" growing in Sugar Creek Reserve. One tree after the other "walks" up the slope, far enough apart to keep branches from entangling, yet close enough to form a continuous display of gigantic strength and overpowering splendor that can be seen at a glance.

May has been gracious with her gifts, using trees for effect. One day the woods were an expanding show of greens and the orchards a hint of white and pink. The next day the undercover of woods, slopes and roadsides was flushed with the lavender-rose of redbud, the orchards lush with the white and pink of cherry, pear and the pervading apple.

Overnight the whole valley had donned its party attire and never before had it looked more alluring. Apple trees spread like comfortable matrons dressed for afternoon tea; the pear trees were colonial maidens, making a bow; the cherry and plum, pretty teenagers wearing their first party dresses.

Birds sang a delirious chorus — robins, thrashers, cardinals, titmice, goldfinches, even a redbreasted grosbeak, and the weak songs of warblers tuned up to celebrate the merry month of May.

I N G

Black rail

The excellent field work of local bird watchers has resulted in an exciting bird record this spring. It was made by James Hill who saw a black rail at Spring Valley.

This is probably one of the rarest birds in our country. Not only is it rare, but it is remarkably difficult to study after it is found, for it can melt from sight out into the wire grass in swampy land.

All rails are escape artists, for they can compress their bodies and can glide in between blades of grass without creating a movement in the vegetation. From this act comes the saying, "as thin as a rail."

Hill got a wonderful look at the little fellow who is five to six inches long, looking as Roger Tory Peterson says, "as big as a young song sparrow with a bobbed tail." What is more newsworthy, he went back the next day and saw it again; he directed another bird watcher to the find and this observer also saw it. Then luck ran out and it hasn't been seen since. But what luck to have a local sight record of this rare, elusive bird!

Let's take a look at the history of this tiny marsh bird. It was discovered in Jamaica in 1760 and was given its scientific name, *creciscus jamacaicensis*, in 1788. But we had to wait until 1836 for it to be found in the United States, when the artist Titian R. Peale showed a collected specimen to Audubon who described and drew it.

It is the most secretive bird alive. Perhaps it is commoner and more widely distributed than is generally supposed, but so far, our records are meager. Its nests are most difficult to find. Usually the bird nests in a tuft of grass where old sere blades are thrust up and out by the new green growth pushing through from below.

The nest is a deep cup with the tall grass serving as cover. A persistent ornithologist seeking to find these nests must examine a multitude of grass clumps from above before he is rewarded in his search. Most often his efforts end in failure.

Once an experienced field man found a nest and watched it for days from every possible approach but never once caught the slightest glimpse of the brooding bird. Not once did a movement of grass indicate that the bird had left, yet when he examined the nest, he found the eggs warm, showing the hen had just left them.

Another record exists of a nest being found with the bird sitting on the eggs. The little creature, startled, darted away and stopped within an inch of the man's toe. At the slightest movement of the observer the bird darted a short distance to a clump of grass and then returned with a remarkable darting movement back to the man's foot. When he stooped to capture it, the little rail flew with the weak, floppy flight of all rails, into the cattails and was never seen again, although the nesting apparently was successful.

Those chosen few who have seen the black rail describe its movements as "darting." Its speed, along with its ability to disappear as if it is practicing magic, makes it one of the most challenging and exciting of all birds to find. That two Dayton birders found it is a gay feather in their caps.

Hilltop view

Modern man, nagged by the heavy responsibilities of daily living, finds it increasingly necessary to find a place of quiet where he can relax physically and regain tranquility of spirit and serenity of mind. Many avenues lead to such a release of tension, a drastic change of pace: a visit to a quiet art gallery, sometimes in the silence of a reading room of a library, meditation in a secluded chapel.

Happily man more and more is finding relaxation in the outdoors experiencing a oneness with nature. As his knowledge of the natural world about him expands, he understands more intelligently his place in the broad plan of nature, even the universe itself, and he becomes content.

Ohio's hill country is an ideal spot for man to cast aside his care, doubt, frustration and to refresh his work-worried body.

The hills stand tree-crowned, calm, eternal. Their rounded peaks reach toward the untroubled blue heavens and their ridges cast a rolling panorama of strength on the horizon as far as the eye can see.

Ohio's hills impress but they do not overwhelm. They are friendly, inviting. Unlike the cold sterility of towering mountains they teem with life; trees of many species yielding nuts and lumber for many purposes. The undercover is rich in berries and wildflowers in exciting variety, all the common species and also many that are rare in form and beauty and scarce in numbers.

The best way to observe hills is from a hilltop. In Shawnee Forest many access roads have been cut throughout the entire reserve. Lookouts at strategic points, where the view is breathtaking, are frequent. Here we see the heroic sweep of the hills, their deep cut ravines. From the lookout we see April reluctantly emerging to the maturity of May. The bright yellow-green on the slopes is the flowering of deciduous trees, gigantic oaks, hickory, walnut, ash and some maple.

From our position we look down on the minute hummingbirds feeding on these high treetop blossoms. In early May this food suffices until later in the month when the hummers appear in our home gardens and find sustenance in the bright flowers growing at this lower level.

Warblers are studied most satisfactorily from this height. They are easily located in the immature foliage and their weak songs are heard to good advantage.

Recently, along the trails of Shawnee we saw a fine list of birds, wildflowers in their perfect innocent beauty. But best of all we felt the serenity, the absolute naturalness, the enveloping peace of the forest. There was only a miminum evidence of man's intrusion in the form of roads, lookouts and trails, and these were made for the protection of wildlife.

In our group was a wise, experienced outdoorsman, Charles Breish, who recently had led a group of young persons on a rugged canoe trip through a Canadian lake-river-forest wilderness area. He summed up our reaction to our Ohio hill wilderness area when he said this of the Canada canoe experience:

"What if records of height or speed are broken? What if kingdoms rise or fall? These are the eternal things; endless sky and water bound together by beauty. We had come to grips with them and had looked upon the face of beauty. We had found peace. Somewhere there must always be a wilderness where man may restore his soul. We must see that it is there, always."

I   N   G

Steadfast hills

The eternal hills! The hills, never changing in their steadfastness, their majesty, their calm serenity. Yet they are ever changing. Every visit there reveals new truth, rediscovered beauty, exciting discovery and expanding knowledge of hill country wildlife.

There comes a deepening appreciation of the vast resources of scenic beauty, the rich variety of plant life, the teeming bird population. Many large butterflies and moths, just emerging from their cocoons, add interest.

An early May weekend spent in Shawnee Forest is a heady experience for the naturalist. All Nature is at its peak. Bird chorus is overwhelming. Birds sing continuously and it takes an expert to isolate and identify individual songs. Most birds are brilliant in color and the pageant of oriole, towhee, cardinal, rose-breasted grosbeak, indigo bunting and brightly colored warblers flying from treetop to treetop is dazzling.

Trails in the forest are really roads, permitting cars to transport us from one advantageous observation post to another. The hardy birdwatcher walks. It is easy to observe birds in the forest. From some cleared lookout at a high elevation you look across the fold of hills and steep gorges into treetops where birds feed. Birds are arriving from their migration north; courtship ecstasy stirs them to outbursts of wondrous music and the air rings with the volume of their singing.

Both the summer and the scarlet tanagers lead the chorus. Their song is lively, melodious and far-carrying. Add to this song strain the exquisite music of wood thrush, indigo bunting, oriole, rose-breasted grosbeak, many warblers, vireos, accented by the loud call of the pileated woodpecker, and you are fully aware that "music swelled the breeze and rang from all the trees," as the stupendous orchestration reverberates through the forest.

Several of our group stood looking across a fold in the hills where a deep gorge had been cut and which ended at our feet. Years ago the slope had been cut for lumber and new scrub growth of underbrush formed a sunny opening. A pair of indigo buntings flew in, alighted on a young treetop and sang. Another flew in, and another, and we realized we were witnessing, were actually in the midst of, the migration of these birds.

We counted 24 buntings, then stopped counting for the flight grew too fast and complicated for us to be accurate.

Migration is a complex phenomenon. It happens all around us, but the movement is so vast that we are not aware of details. It was thrilling beyond words to be part of this cosmic event, when we witnessed the arrival of a single species in form of this merry little songster.

Woodpeckers

How exciting it would be if we could turn back the passing of time and roam the undisturbed primeval forests of colonial days.

The early naturalists that reached America from the Old World were amazed at the complexity and infinite variety of our flora and fauna.

John and William Bartram, two native botanists, made a comfortable living by sending botanical specimens and seeds to collectors in Europe. Because they were alert observers of the outdoors, they also contributed valuable, accurate information to those engaged in the work of classifying and describing our American birds.

When Alexander Wilson, a poor weaver from Scotland, decided to try his fortune in America, he disembarked at New Castle and walked overland to his destination in Philadelphia, a trek of 35 miles. He was entranced with the beauty of the birds he saw along the forest trail, and determined to learn the birds of this strange new land.

Later he wrote his famous *Birds of America*, thus earning the title, father of American ornithology.

Two spectacular birds completely captivated the attention of the naturalists of Wilson's day: the ivory billed woodpecker, one of the largest denizens of the forest, and the pileated woodpecker, large as a crow.

The ivory billed woodpecker is now thought to be extinct. The pileated woodpecker, a few years ago, was considered on its way out, too. It was a bird of the virgin forest and since it was gone, the bird, showing a lack of ability to adapt itself to changing conditions in its environment, was thought to be in a precarious state.

Today, however, we have reason to believe that this bird is increasing in numbers. As the second growth trees reach maturity, the pileated is seen with greater frequency throughout its wide range.

This large woodpecker is handsome, indeed: body predominantly black, white wing bars, prominent white stripes on neck and head and proudly holding aloft a vivid red crest.

For years this enormous, handsome woodpecker escaped my observation. I could be on a field trip where others saw it, but not I.

Then came the memorable day when we found a nesting pair feeding their demanding young about 30 feet up in a large hickory tree at Fort Hill.

Since then I once heard the woodpecker on the grounds of the Dayton Museum of Natural History. Its loud cry, much like that of the flicker, reverberated through the woods and was heard as the bird flew north out of hearing range along the Stillwater.

I have also seen it in our Montgomery County Parks. There are records of its having been seen at the Englewood Reserve and there are several successful nesting records for it at Sugar Grove Reserve.

Our sturdy early settler ancestors had colorful colloquial names for this large woodpecker: Log Cock, Cock o'the Woods, Lord God Woodpecker and Wood Kate, to name a few.

I   N   G

Happy Skeeter

I have never been fond of cats. They look at you, cold and condescending, as if you are not there. They deliberately twine their sinuous bodies around your ankles as if they are alleviating an unreachable itch. When this happens to me the muscles at the back of my neck crawl, my stomach twists into a knot and it takes all my self control to keep from screaming.

In spite of my phobia, I am, from a distance, able to regard cats with an honest appraisal. I recognize their feline grace. Little kittens playing together make a charming picture. Then, too, I know that cats play an important role in the broad plan of nature. All cats, from the fierce tiger down to the common house cat, have highly developed hunting instincts. They prey on many forms of wildlife and thus affect a natural population control.

Domestic cats are particularly unpopular when they catch birds at feeding stations in our home grounds. Their hunting is an important link in the food chain and while the human is indignant when a cat pounces on a bird he is protecting, he should remember that a cat seldom captures a healthy, well-coordinated, aware bird. The old, inept, sick birds, victims of the cat's hunting skill, are a part of a wise, humane act that disposes of those unable to make an escape. Even so, I don't want cats to touch me. I consider such effrontery an act of feline harassment.

And then I met Skeeter. Skeeter, a beautiful young calico cat, was dropped off in front of my neighbor's house. She was a blend of black, white and orange, her belly pure white. Her black tail was as long as her body. She held it erect and the tip curved like the curved hand grip on a walking stick. She carried it proudly aloft like a flag.

I watched Skeeter from my kitchen window. She was so happy, so playful, so lithe and graceful, so inventive in entertaining herself that I felt my cold anti-cat heart melt to a strange warmth. She took great leaping bounds across the lawn, concluding such exercise by running up the trunk of a great tree with the agility of a squirrel.

She swung from one branch to another on the old lilac bush like a professional gymnast. She would sneak up on the ground feeding birds crawling on her belly, ready to pounce at the right moment using the privet hedge as cover. I never saw her catch a bird.

Skeeter had a bowl of food and a tin pan for milk or water in a protected corner near the back door of her home, but she chose to get her drink of water from my bird fountain. A large stone is imbedded in a small rock garden near the fountain. Skeeter squeezed under the fence, placed her hind legs on the rock, stretched her body like a rubber band, held on to the brim of the fountain with her front paws and drank her fill.

Skeeter seemed to anticipate Fridays when my neighbor took me to market. She'd squeeze under the fence and come into my yard, on our return, to watch us unload the car and take in the groceries. Then she leaped into the car, settled herself on the front seat and drove home in style — a short drive, just next door.

Dear, happy little Skeeter with the erect, crooked black tail held proudly aloft like a flag! One unhappy day last week she was killed by a car in front of her house.

Perfect days

June! Then, if ever, come perfect days. The perfection is mirrored in many ways, in near-at-home places. We do not need to go to faraway places to see her beauty or perfection.

"He is a thoroughly good naturalist who knows his own parish thoroughly." We find sound proof of this philosophy in Prof. William Werthner's excellent book, *Some American Trees*. The trees discussed and photographed by this teacher-naturalist of Steele High School were all found in the Dayton area.

The mystic English poet William Blake once wrote that the stay-at-home who looks on nature with sympathetic understanding "sees a world in a grain of sand, and Heaven in a wildflower."

There are many large, exciting gardens in the Dayton area. Perhaps Mrs. John Aull's garden heads the list, and through her generosity it is open daily to the public. June makes it a place of rare beauty, serenity and peace and does much to heal the visitor's frayed tensions and renew his spirit.

Yet, the small home garden can have the same effect, serve the same purpose. Here in his own "parish," man can tune in on the eternal verities, create his own Eden.

This June is the culmination of all natural effort. I have seldom seen such rich lushness in foliage of all kinds. In a fine woods I tramped lately I stood on a slight rise and looked across at the undercover. It seemed like a jungle — tangled, close-grown, leaves almost twice normal size. A patch of May apple produced leaves at least 15 inches across.

Foliage on trees is so dense shadows appear solid, black. There is no laciness in the shade that slants across the lawn. Van Dyke, in his poem *God of the Open Air*, lists among the many things he "holds of dearest worth," "shadows of clouds that swiftly pass."

The play of June's sunlight and dark shade, sunlight and black shadow, on open space make delightful contrasts.

Van Dyke prizes, too, "comfort of grass, music of birds, murmur of little rills." Grass is probably the most important plant family in our world. From some of its members come food for millions of people — rice, corn, wheat, oats, etc. Grass is the main source of food for wild and domestic animals. It is persistent, and when it takes over the flower beds the gardener is apt to forget its universal importance and find small comfort in the task of rescuing the flowers from its smothering.

Music of birds and murmur of little rills go hand in hand. Birds love water, and their numbers increase in land through which a happy rill finds it way. The brook at Aullwood is the closest small stream I can visit and it is dear to my heart. It murmurs musically under its breath for some distance in its course, then sings a gay soprano as it descends a way before it tumbles giddily to form a wee waterfall. Then it shouts a rollicking medley of soprano, alto and high tenor vocalizing.

All along Aullwood brook the birds give joyous greeting to its singing water. They join their own sweet tunes to its liquid music — robin, brown thrasher, wren, vireo, cardinal, Baltimore oriole, bluebird, redwing, towhee, chittering swift, goldfinch and bunting — with woodpeckers adding their bass notes through their drumming. Music of birds, murmur of little rills add another perfection to June's perfect days.

I N G

Summer

The little bird sits at his door in the sun
Atilt like a blossom among the leaves,
And lets his illumined being o'er run
With the deluge of summer it receives.
His mate feels the eggs beneath her wings
And the heart in her dumb breast flutters and sings.
He sings to the wide world,
And she to her nest.
In the nice ear of Nature, which song is the best?

James Russell Lowell

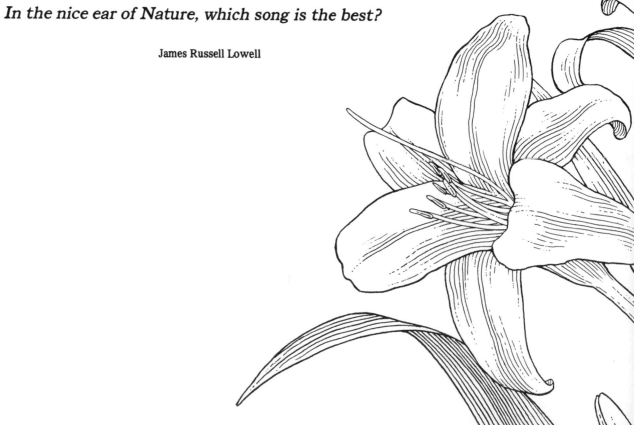

A bit of whimsy

The Lord God felt very happy this day. He had been working on a new planet. It was finished now, and He felt He could relax.

First the Lord God had separated the darkness from the light. Now this was really hard to manage — darkness wanted to go first without taking turns and light insisted on staying up late, longer than the Lord God wanted it to. At last they both behaved, and the Lord God took the next step.

The next day the work went well. He divided the vapor that covered the new planet and made the sky. He colored it blue. He made fluffy white clouds that played tag all over its blue depth. It pleased the Lord God so well He gave it a special name, heaven. He gave a name to the darkness, too, calling it evening, and the light He called morning.

Water was everywhere. Now the Lord God loved water, but He didn't want His new planet all water, so He pushed a little to one side and there was dry land.

"Good," said the Lord God. "Now we're getting somewhere." He was enjoying himself. Each new piece of work He finished He gave a name. He called the water sea and the land earth.

Earth started to work right away and covered itself with grasses and tall trees that had great hollow branches. The Lord God was pleased, but He knew that green plants needed more in order to grow, so the next day He set the great sun in the heaven to give light and heat during the day, and

He put a pale moon and twinkling stars in the sky to make the night beautiful.

Now the Lord God felt happy, indeed. He looked at his new planet and smiled. It was very splendid and hung like a great silver pear in the sky. It had been hard work pushing things around and arranging them in order. He felt a little tired and stiff, so He decided to do a little light work on His new planet this fourth day.

Here He had made a sky like a huge blue dome, land covered with grass and tall trees, wide stretches of water that danced in the sunlight, but somehow it was too quiet, lifeless. So the Lord God made fish and whales and other animals that loved the water and put them in the seas.

He made animals that liked the land covered with grasses and tall trees. He made all kinds of singing birds, gave them wings and the gift of song and they flew into the air and over land and sea, making the new planet ring with the joy of their music.

The Lord God looked at it all and was pleased. He laughed aloud and clapped His hands and cried, "It is good!"

He walked along a sandy beach where tiny waves from the seas lapped the shore. It was empty. The Lord God had a loving thought. He made a small bird to run along the sand. Its legs were long so it could walk in the shallow water, but it soon became bogged down in the wet sand. The waves washed over it. It struggled to get up, but

S   U   M

the waves swept it back again and again. It was afraid.

"Ka-de-a-dee-ka-dede-de," it sputtered, coughed and gasped. The Lord God scooped it up in His hands. He looked it over carefully: "It's just a problem of weight and balance," He decided. He made the legs a little longer and more slender. He drew the toes out long and thin. "There, little fellow," said the Lord God, giving it a loving pat on its back near its tail, "Try walking again."

Off ran the little long-legged bird. Now its feet left prints in the sand, but they didn't sink in and get dirty. It felt happy. It ran and shouted, "Ka-dee-ka-dee," as it played with the tiny waves, chasing them as they flowed out to sea, running away from them as they came rushing back to land.

What a busy bird it was, and pretty, too, its body brown as the wet sand, its breast white as the foam on the waves. A black necklace around its neck gave it an all-dressed-up look. On its back near its tail where the Lord God had given it a loving pat was a spot of orange the color of the rising sun.

When the little bird grew up, all his children looked like him. They all are happy and noisy, shouting as they fly, shouting as they feed, shouting to each other, "ka-dee, ka-dee." So now this bird, especially loved by the Lord God, is called killdeer.

M   E   R

Forest trails

In Ohio all roads south eventually lead to the hills. Some throughways run straight and level, for the practical engineers that built them cut through and flattened the hills, thinking only of saving time, getting from one place to another in a hurry.

Some roads, however, follow ancient trails and wind around the foot of the hills, with a tumbling stream alongside and a glimpse of narrow valleys where hill people have taken to farming. These are the roads we like to follow.

On the way to Shawnee Forest, one of Ohio's largest and most beautiful parks, we see the first lift of the hills as we approach Hillsboro. They rise along the horizon, fold after fold, with an occasional peak emphasizing their grandeur. Sometimes if rain threatens, we see water vapor rise, form a small cloud that merges with the larger cloud mass on the hill's crest. The wind accelerates, pushing along the cloud now heavy with moisture, and soon it descends in a quick shower.

The ponderous extent of the hills is relieved by the forests they carry on their backs. Now the forest trees are in bloom and their flowering is a filigree of airy lightness against the hillside's solid strength. Every nuance of greenish yellow is captured in their flowers. This diversity of color saves Ohio's hills from appearing forbidding.

The trails reveal the richness of wildlife preserved and protected in this vast state park. The trees are singing posts for a countless number of birds. Two birds, brilliant in color and song, are the scarlet and summer tanagers. The summer tanager is all-over red and the scarlet tanager is a glowing scarlet bird with black wings and tail.

Warblers and vireos sing from the treetops. They feed on tiny caterpillars found on emerging foliage and keep it clean and near-perfect. Some warblers prefer the undercover in the ravines and one bold warbler, the biggest of his tribe — the yellowbreasted chat — gives a fine performance for us in the heavy vegetation of a fence row.

Wild flowers are fantastic in this place. They are abundant and by growing in masses make stunning effects along the way. Many that grow in Shawnee are found in our area but many do not grow farther north. Iris verna, a blue iris only three inches tall, blankets the high slopes.

The rose-colored moccasin flower, an orchid, is abundant, perfect. How good it is to know it can grow here undisturbed.

Then Nature, tempering her largesse, granted us the privilege of finding single specimens of two of her rare treasures. First, the showy orchis, perfect, exquisite, petite, pink and white about six inches tall.

The second was the very rare whorled pogonia, an orchid. It was found only by chance in the gray-brown leaf mold by an alert observer (not I). At the tip of a slender six-inch stem was a tiny greenish yellow flower with three one-inch extending brown sepals. The whorled leaves below the bloom gave the plant the effect of motion. Only one plant was found. How fragile is the assurance of survival of this rare bit of wild beauty!

S   U   M

Whippoorwill

The whippoorwill is a mysterious bird of the night. When other nocturnal sounds have stilled to the persistent thin high-pitched insect voices, out of the darkness comes the harried command of this bird, "whippoorwill."

Over and over is the call repeated as if he were obsessed by some inner compulsion to belabor poor Will.

It is a creature that many hear but seldom see. After long years of bird watching, I have heard this bird sing many times in many places, but I have seen it only twice. It is an excellent refutation of the old admonition that there is virtue in "being seen but not heard."

Even though the whippoorwill carries on his affairs in the darkness of night, there is nothing sinister about the bird. The rhythm of his calling is pleasant and if he were bent on evil he wouldn't be so imprudent as to advertise his whereabouts. For the whip repeats his call many times, in fact, one wonders when he takes a breath.

A neighbor once told John Burroughs he'd heard a whippoorwill call over 200 times without taking a breath. Mr. Burroughs took this tall tale with a grain of salt until he, himself, had the remarkable field experience of hearing a whippoorwill "deliver poor Will 1,088 blows."

Once I saw two half-grown young whippoorwills in the fine old woods, now destroyed, at Calvary Cemetery. They were fluttering about like fallen brown leaves in the undercover, unable to fly, proving that the strange birds had nested there.

The second time I saw the bird, one flew across the trail in front of my husband and me as we walked through a woods at dusk at Englewood Reserve. It moved like a noiseless shadow on its soft dark wings, more spirit than bird, and alighted, lengthwise, on a low horizontal branch, so close we could almost touch it.

Its dark somber brown plumage was relieved by streaks of off-white and a thin narrow white band that curved upward under the throat. But the conclusive identification character was the bulky head that seemingly has no neck. The cavernous mouth measures two inches across. The muscles controlling the jaws are weak and the bird flies with its heavily bristled mouth open, practically flying into its food.

I'm certain there's nothing superstitious about my associating this bird with severe storms, but the few times I've heard it in my own neighborhood, its calling preceded thunderstorms, one attended by heavy rains and wind that felled two well-loved old apple trees in our yard.

A few weeks ago on a camping trip to Adams County's beautiful hill country the whippoorwill's call conjured up a storm that made the night miserable with thunder, lightning and an inch of rain that fell in about half an hour's time.

M   E   R

Hedge apples

June lays her warm hand on the land. It is a strengthening, encouraging warmth that brings the tender young growth of April and May to a self-confident maturity. In the fields straight rows of corn stand in military precision, the yellow-green of spring deepened to the sturdy blue-green of summer. Soybean rows are straight as if measured by some gigantic yardstick.

Wheat fields sigh in the wind and ripple in undulating grace over the wide expanse of their planting. Their green now glints with a hint of gold as the seed heads ripen toward July's harvest.

There is no ragged beauty in the sterile fence rows that enclose America's broad Midwestern farmlands today. Modern farming is big business, strictly a dollar-and-cents operation with land cultivated close to every wire fence line, not an inch wasted. Gone forever is the old-fashioned fence of hedge apple, that tough, glossy leafed shrub cut back periodically by the hard working farmer to make a hedge that never reached the height of handsome trees it was capable of becoming. In the hedge row's protection sprang up a host of colorful wildflowers, bouncing Bet, all the pretty wild asters, campion, beardstongue, cinquefoil, goldenrod, milkweed and many other flowers that made the roadside a thing of interest and beauty.

Hedge apple is a common name for Osage Orange, a tree common to the Red River Valley and used widely by the Osage Indians for bows and for a yellow dye made from the wood. Since it made a good hedge, it became a popular substitute for the old stake-and-rider fences on pioneer farms.

According to Prof. Werthner in his book, *Some American Trees*, Dayton was headquarters for a patented method for setting out Osage Orange cuttings and training them into hedges.

Stout thorns grew on untrimmed hedges and served as pantries for the migrant shrike, a handsome bird of the open country, to store its food. Shrikes are about robin size, soft gray with white underparts and black on the tail. A dashing black mask spans the beak and extends through the eyes. These birds catch their food, small mice, meadow voles and large insects, like the grasshopper, and impale them on the thorns, which make a handy storage device. When more economical wire fencing replaced the wasteful hedgerow the bold buccaneer shrike also disappeared.

Many fine individual specimen Osage Orange trees can be found in our valley. Several large, wide spreading trees are found at Englewood Reserve and Aullwood Center. The fruit is a large, rough ball, yellow green and very striking against the glossy, dark green foliage. In winter squirrels break open the "apples" and eat the coarse fiber. Accepting gratefully the squirrels' service in making the food available, goldfinches and titmice also feed on the fruit.

June "tries the earth if it be in tune." June is a gentle month, yet a month that stirs with the strong natural rhythm of seeding, the expanding leaf, developing fruit in orchard and vineyard, the nestling flexing its wings and gliding from the nest, turtle and snake eggs hatching, a deafening "peeper" chorus in the wet woods, the chimney swift zooming down the chimney where it nests.

"Whether we look or whether we listen, we hear life murmur or see it glisten." June, once considered a romantic month of moonlight and roses dedicated to young lovers, is really a busy, steady, motherly month that manages to do her duty without fanfare.

S   U   M

Fledgling robin

An unblinking young robin, with juvenile black spots standing out like huge freckles on its brown breast, balanced precariously on a dead twig rising from the brush pile.

He was unafraid as I worked in the garden close by, not knowing or caring that he was slowing down my work.

How could I flush so confident a young fellow, looking out on his brave new world, by tossing weeds on the haven he'd chosen for a lookout?

As I watched, he awkwardly glided down into the grass, gave a few loud food squawks and almost immediately his mother came and fed him.

He was one of countless numbers of fledglings now being launched into adult life. For quite a while they are dependent on the old birds for food and protection until wings become strong enough to sustain flight and they are capable of finding food and feeding themselves.

This period is a time of danger for the young bird and concern for the old ones. It is a time when natural enemies prey on the helpless young. But a greater danger lies in their contact with man. I have received many complaints about children wantonly teasing and killing young birds that cannot make a quick getaway in flight.

And then compassionate adults, finding a young bird and not seeing the old birds about, conclude that the fledgling is deserted or the parent bird dead. They pick up the bird, take it inside, put it in a box and try to raise it. From that moment the bird is doomed. Why?

Does a human know how the parent feeds its young? By pushing food down its throat or by regurgitation of predigested food? Does a human know the technique of getting a baby bird to swallow automatically? It is impossible for a human to simulate the regurgitation method of feeding.

What should the bird be fed? The first few days of its life, parents feed many species of young birds predigested food by regurgitating it. Then follows a diet of caterpillars, soft insects and wild fruits.

How can a human possibly find enough of this type of food to feed a demanding young bird every few minutes? It eats tremendous amounts of food and most humans can't take time from other duties to feed the bird as often as its need demands. Any substitute food results in sickness and death.

If by some fluke it survives, it will not lead a normal life as it will be dependent on its benefactor(?) for safety and companionship and may never assume its natural place among its own wild kind.

It is illegal to have a migratory bird in your possession. So the only thing you should do when you find a young bird you think is orphaned or deserted, is to see that it is not harmed by cruel humans and then LEAVE IT ALONE.

Virgin woods

The groves were God's first temples . . .
. . . now they stand massy, and tall and dark,
Fit shrine for humble worshipper to hold
Communion with his Maker.

— Bryant

This feeling of communion and reverence was never more poignantly experienced than it was recently when I had an opportunity to tramp through a fine old woods on the Schaeffer farm in Preble County. In this 40-acre stand there are magnificent specimens of trees that probably were saplings when Columbus discovered America. Such remnants of true forest are rarely found in our state today.

Towering red, white and chinkapin or yellow oak trees, massive with the rugged strength characteristic of the oak, indicate age, yet show no debilitating signs of aging. Hickories of all species are found in these woods, with outstanding specimens of the shell bark and mockernut. Ash trees grow to great height and girth. Wild cherries rise straight and to an unusual height.

Several black gums, tall, slender trees, grow here. This is the tree that turns a flaming red in the fall. I like the Indian name, Tupelo, for this distinctive tree that is not abundant anywhere throughout its range.

Some enormous hard maples spread their broad branches in this forest. It is interesting to note that this species is showing an aggressiveness lacking in other kinds of trees, as the under canopy is crowded with young maple saplings.

It is the beech trees, however, that stir me most deeply. Many, judging by their great girth and height, are ancient giants. Many, perhaps middle-aged, stand in their straight strength and perfection, so impervious to time, weather, proximity to their neighbors, the eccentricities of nature itself (Indians solemnly believed that beeches are never

struck by lightning), that they seem to be set apart.

The beech is a tree of great antiquity. Its fossilized forms indicate age in eons of time and it has been associated with man since before the written history of his existence.

Beeches may well have been God's first temples, for they often stand in groves, woods within a woods. The smooth, light-gray trunks show through the forest's greenery and locate and identify the trees immediately. How arrogant, how self-composed they appear beside the other trees with their struggling twists and turns of trunks and branches. It is as if the beech is an aristocrat "in plebian forest crowd in which it finds itself."

Beech branches extend widespread from the trunk. Leaves, lustrous bronze-green, are pointed with serrate edges and straight, pronounced veins. The fruit, two three-cornered chestnut colored nuts enclosed in prickly burs, is tasty-sweet and sought after by small boys and squirrels as soon as the burs burst open after the first frosts.

Our host told us that the beech makes superior firewood, for its tough, close-grained wood burns long and gives off a good heat. Early settlers used it chiefly for this purpose, for it was too tough to handle with primitive tools. Later, when machine tools were used, many articles were made from its wood: clothespins, bobbins, brush backs, tool handles, clothes horses, paving blocks. Beechwood makes the best barrels ever manufactured and because the wood is tasteless, it makes excellent ice cream beaters, churns, wooden bowls and kitchenware.

"Today I have grown taller from walking with the trees," a poet once wrote. Alas, it isn't possible to have this continuing experience in our changing natural world. But I know the aesthetic and spiritual experience of visiting this fabulous bit of forest will sustain me until I can walk in the presence of the calm strength of great trees again.

Mullein

This day we idly followed a trail we seldom trod, and gold was found at its sudden turning. Not the gold that can be bartered at the mart in exchange for material needs, but the gold that enriches the spirit and brings wealth of mind where experiences and impressions are stored in a mental file to be referred to over and over again.

The way was cool and shaded and moist from the fog that was lifting rapidly toward the journeying sun. There was bird song, there was the brassy drone of insect voices, there were the intriguing plants coming into midsummer bloom. Then abruptly the trail was gone! And there was the gold!

Before our incredulous gaze was a veritable city of spires and skyscrapers and lesser structures stretching out into the distance. It was a city of Great Mullein, whose sturdy stalks rose like gleaming candles alight with yellow flame. They were all green and in full bloom.

How tall they were! They towered above the more than six-foot Senior Ornithologist. In one direction they blended into the background of the grassy slope of the Englewood dam; in another their backdrop was the dense green woods.

It was an amazing sight. Never before had we seen more than a dozen of these plants growing together in a close patch. Here they grew for a distance comparable to a city square, plant after plant, stalwart, erect, perfect. We estimated that there must be around 500 of them.

Mullein is one of our commonest wild plants. It has a long list of folk names, for it is well known throughout its range, particularly in the eastern part of our country, and in our own locality where it is very appropriately called velvet plant.

The basal and stem leaves are covered so compactly with hairy filaments that they create the effect of softest velvet to the touch.

There is an exciting relationship between this plant and other forms of wildlife. These hairy filaments are cherished by the wee hummingbird who uses them to line her nest.

A gay flock of goldfinches clung to the flower stalks and feasted on the diminutive seeds. Several downy woodpeckers were pecking on the long stems, evidently finding some insect fare that they enjoyed heartily. In fact they were loath to leave the plants at all and flew on only when we were within a very few feet of them.

The air buzzed with insects: bumble bees lumbered about, carpenter and honeybees found the insignificant blossoms to their liking; wasps and flies of all sorts were busily at work and butterflies were having a heyday.

On a trip to Europe, John Burroughs was surprised to find our common mullein cultivated in a garden. We wonder at his surprise, for we know it grows wild in England, even though it thrives best in the hot, semi-arid lands of the Mediterranean. For was not this plant, *Verbascum Thapsus*, named for the town of Thapsus in Sicily, or could it have originated in Thapsus of Africa?

We know that some of its seeds, of no more substance than flecks of black pepper, reached American shores in ballast from early sailing ships and since then the plant has marched across our continent.

S   U   M

Eternal hope

Alexander Pope must have had farmers and gardeners in mind when he wrote in his *Essay on Man,* "Hope springs eternal in the human breast."

Last year, after seasonal weather extremes that ran the gamut of a record-breaking cold winter, to a summer-like spring, to a searing hot summer attended by a prolonged drought, I lost all hope as a gardener. After seeing my flowers die as if cooked by a diabolic chef, I decided I'd have my flower borders plowed under and planted to grass.

Another record-breaking winter kept us housebound and then there descended upon us the most miraculous spring of the past decade. Ideal weather caused flowers we thought dead to pop through the soil with breathless beauty and vigor. Some, like my old tree peony, lamented as gone, reached into the latent stamina inherent in the plant and staged a resurrection that would put to shame any doubting Thomas.

Any hasty decision I had made to discontinue growing flowering plants vanished as quickly as dandelion fluff in a brisk breeze. That old eternal hope sprang up again as if it had never faltered and I've been deep in gardening ever since the first valiant snowdrop bloomed, surrounded by snow reluctant to melt.

But gardening is not all beer and skittles. You must have more than hope. A huge dose of patience plus a stout back and conditioned muscles go a long way toward achieving an attractive garden.

I've always firmly believed that every living thing, from the microscopic plant or animal to the largest, has a purpose in the broad plan of creation and, consequently I have respect, even reverence, for all forms of life.

But as a gardener, with a finite mind and a patience that has its limits, I find myself questioning the necessity for the existence of some weeds that mean trouble. They actually grow in winter under 40 inches of snow and in continuing below-zero temperatures. This gives them a start on the useful plants of the flower and vegetable gardens and adds to the problems of their cultivation.

One weed is the sneaky ground ivy that slithers over the ground on an elongated stem that sends rootlets into the soil at intervals, making it a nuisance which is almost impossible to control. I'm sure its intended function is to be a ground cover and an aid in preventing soil erosion, but I have no such problems in my garden. Nevertheless, it is perverse and "wants to do its own thing." In my garden it takes over flower beds, rock gardens and grass, leaving the lawn looking ragged and unkempt.

Ground ivy, however, is an angel compared to quack grass. I can find no justification for its existence. Quack grass is a maverick in the highly respected order of grasses, some of which, like corn, wheat, rice, etc., feed the people of the earth. Other grasses keep our world green and provide food for many animals, both wild and domesticated.

Quack grass produces long, jointed, fleshy roots that are strong enough to grow straight through a bulb, weakening it so it produces inferior flowers. It is coarse and smothers other competitive plants. It is almost impossible to control, for if one root remains in the ground it will send up a new plant. When and if I get to heaven I must have a talk with the Creator about quack grass.

M   E   R

Chipmunks

Early in our marriage, the Senior Ornithologist planted several dozen crocus bulbs in a spot in our yard that later became our pocket-handkerchief-sized wildflower garden. But when spring came, only eight or ten blossoms appeared.

"The chipmunks probably ate the bulbs," the S.O. said in explaining the crocus crop failure.

We decided then that chipmunks are handsomer than crocuses are beautiful, and far more interesting. Their glossy, warm, brown, fur-clad bodies — with five black stripes from shoulder to rump and a white stripe between two black ones on each flank — give the little fellows a jaunty air.

The tawny color on the sides grades to clear white on the belly, adding to the chipmunk's good looks. And his flat tail is not bushy, but the hair grows thick on it and he holds it gaily aloft like a brave flag.

Chipmunks are tiny, alert, curious bundles of energy, averaging 8-10 inches from the tip of the nose to the tip of the tail and weighing from three to five ounces.

They live in burrows whose entrances are about two inches in diameter and lead straight down about nine inches before tapering off a few feet to comfortable living quarters with a living-bedroom, storeroom and bathroom.

We've always had chipmunks in our garden. Some years they were more numerous than others, the controlling factor being whether or not we had a dog — not necessarily a hunter, just an easily excited barker. And, when our neighbors had a cat, the two served as natural controls, keeping the chipmunk population in check.

One year when there were no cats or dogs to intimidate the chipmunks, they moved into the entire neighborhood, but were never a nuisance, just fun.

The chipmunk is a choice wild creature normally living in sunny edges of woodlots, thickets and "people" gardens. He gives people an opportunity to observe a wild animal close-up, for he is active during the day, while most small mammals are nocturnal.

On my home grounds, he's entertained us with his endearing ways, like drinking from my water fountain. He grips the rim with his hind feet and stretches his body forward as if it were made of elastic. Or like quarreling with the catbird for ripened berries on the high-bush cranberry — the animal stuffing his cheek pouches to bursting, the catbird gobbling down one berry after the other, and each hurling unprintable insults at the other in his native tongue.

Chipmunks move with exquisite coordination and speed. They love the woodpiles they find in our yards — good

retreats, for they have many enemies. My rock wall is sheer delight, since it has many crannies where they can explore and exercise their curiosity.

The catless, dogless summer was the time an enterprising chipmunk robbed a flower bed in my garden of 78 of seven dozen tulip bulbs. I watched the little scamp unerringly dig up a bulb, slide under the wire fence to his burrow on my neighbor's place, then return for more. Perhaps it was my imagination, but he appeared so smug, so pleased with himself for being so provident for the winter, that he seemed to swagger. In spite of my aggravation for the loss of my tulip bulbs, I had to chuckle at his impudence and ingenuity.

Chipmunks belong to the order of rodents which includes woodchucks, porcupines, beavers, rabbits, hares, rats and mice. Two rodents, the house mouse and Norway rat — both aliens, brought to our continent in colonial days in holds of sailing vessels trading in European ports — have given, because of their unhealthy and repulsive habits, the entire order a black name. Biologically ignorant people have tarred all rodents with a black brush for the sins of two family black sheep and considered all rodents subjects for extermination.

The tiny chipmunk is a useful as well as a good-looking, interesting fellow. Let me count the ways: In tunneling his burrow, he aerates the soil, checking rain and snow runoffs. He eats food destructive to plant life, including snails, slugs and caterpillars. Wild cherry and hackberry seeds are buried, resulting in new tree growth. He eats nuts from the beech, walnut, hickory and oak trees often burying some that result in extended forests. He is a powerful disseminator of wild seeds and bulbs through movement of soil in his tunneling. The extension of many species of wildflowers is credited to this tireless little worker.

And he is an important link in the food chain of the wildlife community, for he is a source of food for carnivorous animals and birds of prey. He is often attacked by snakes and weasels in his own burrow. This natural control keeps him from becoming a problem to humans.

It is sad, even tragic, when the human family alienates itself so completely from its natural environment that the presence of a beautiful little animal weighing less than a half-pound causes unreasoning panic, which leads to the urge to exterminate, to end the existence of a beautiful, useful, exciting creature. The methods of extermination used — often incredibly cruel and inhumane — create in the compassionate human a feeling of frustration, sadness and despair.

M   E   R

Butterflies

When June advances into July, she hands over to this hot month a task she had already begun. It involves a complicated feature of summer wildlife which adds up to a varied display of beauty and an interest in the way the beauty was created.

In late June and during July when more robust and deeply colored flowers start blooming in fields and cultivated gardens, insect life is stimulated and increases. Then brilliant butterflies and moths appear on the bright hued flowers, the butterfly during the daytime, the moths at night. They add color, excitement and movement to outdoor summer.

In recent years when chemical sprays have been used indiscriminately along country roads and in private gardens, butterflies have diminished to an alarming degree. All who love a natural beauty in our environment are bereft at the loss of this resource of beauty. It is an unnecessary waste and a glaring example of how people of intelligence and sensitivity are led astray by not understanding the life history of these exquisite creatures.

Adult butterflies are fragile, their wings delicate. Their loveliness is quickly destroyed by the clumsiness of human touch and handling. Yet they are able to weather storms and some species are tough enough to take long migrations or to hibernate through long, cold winters.

The life history, or metamorphosis, of butterflies and moths is perhaps well known to those who read this column but a very elementary discussion of this phenomenon might be helpful as a review. The adult female lays eggs on a host plant. She instinctively selects the plant the caterpillar, or larva, that hatches from the egg will find compatible. It will enjoy it, will be able to digest it and will develop rapidly upon feeding upon it. For example, the Monarch butterfly lays her eggs on the common milkweed.

The larva eats until it reaches the next stage of its metamorphosis. The larva stage is when the insect does the most damage and when sprays are used for its destruction. The larvae of our largest, most brilliantly beautiful butterflies are not numerous enough to damage food crops. They are victims of injudicious spraying, nonetheless.

At the end of the feeding period the larvae go into the resting period in which the butterfly larva makes a chrysalis to protect the soft dormant caterpillar. Moths weave cocoons for this purpose. Eventually the adult insect emerges from its chrysalis or cocoon as a butterfly or moth and starts on its adult life.

By some happy circumstance, I've seen more butterflies, both species and individuals, so far this summer than I've seen for several years. I've spent every morning the past week at Aullwood Center

S   U   M

and the butterflies have staged a splendid show. I'm certain they will reach a peak the first 10 days in July when the marsh and prairie flowers come into bloom.

Swallowtails are always exciting for their size, color, manner of flight. Tiger, zebra and the equally beautiful blue swallowtails were seen. Swallowtails are identified by the tail-like extension on the lower wing that gives the butterfly the grace of the swallow, since it resembles the long tail feathers of those birds.

The great spangled fritillary spread its wide brown wings at the edge of the woods bordering the prairie and the red admiral and painted lady basked in the sun along the same path. Graylings were the most numerous species. They fly erratically and stop frequently to rest, closing their wings tightly without flexing. They're friendly and unafraid, often alighting on children, much to their delight.

Butterflies sip nectar from flowers through a tube called proboscis. Edmund Spenser, an Elizabethan poet, described their sipping thus:

Now this, now that, he tasteth tenderly,
Yet none of them he rudely doth disorder.

After mating and laying their eggs, the butterflies soon die. That they are seen into the early warm days of autumn is due to their producing several broods.

M   E   R

Marsh life

A vast marsh that covers acres of terrain lush with vegetation that grows best in wetlands, with occasional stretches of open water that eventually give way to forests of exotic trees and undercover, is an exciting, even awesome ecological environment.

But a tiny marsh you can contemplate at a glance is a jewel of perfect cut. It is rare, too, sometimes seen by happy accident, sometimes sought out because a friend told you where to find it.

I came upon a wee marsh after following an easy trail. Its small water area, shrunken by the long drought, was criss-crossed by muskrat trails. Crawdad castles drained in the sun and there came the "plunk" of a frog as it jumped in the water at my approach.

Beyond the pond the woods looked dark and cool but on both sides, open to the light and heat that shimmered over its surface, grew the feathery queen-of-the-prairie and the tall spikes of purple loosestrife. Both showy flowers are at the peak of their bloom now.

Queen-of-the-prairie, an exquisite pink, stands about six feet high, the long stem topped by a spreading cluster of flowers. The stems on each floweret are unusually long and give the really robust plant the effect of fragile laciness.

Masses of the sturdy loosestrife are rosy lavender and blend beautifully with the pink of the queen-of-the-prairie. The rose of swamp milkweed is somewhat overpowered in competition but its contribution is important to the vivid color glistening under the brazen sky.

The entire marsh was in motion, set, not particularly by the hot, lazy breeze but by the movement of a multitude of wings, the soft fluttering wings of multicolored butterflies, darting wings of dragonflies, the purposeful wing-flight of bees, wasps, beetles, flies. All appeared giddy, hovering over the flowers, drinking nectar from their fresh, breath-taking beauty.

This animated scene proved that although much depleted in numbers, butterflies have not entirely disappeared, for the diversity of species here was bewildering. I easily identified skippers, satyrs, both color phases of the tiger swallowtail and the blue swallowtail, sulfur, cabbage, violet tip, fritillary, monarch, red admiral and the blue-eyed graylings making courtship flights and mating.

Goldfinches, indigo buntings, and a yellowthroat provided a musical background for their feast, the only discordant note coming from a disgruntled green heron who uttered an indignant "quark" at the intrusion in his Eden.

This small swamp, actively supporting all forms of wildlife, plant, insect, reptile, amphibian, fish, bird, mammal and teeming microscopic life in the pond, is within easy access. It is one of the exciting habitats found at Aullwood Audubon Center, a true sanctuary where all forms of wildlife are recognized, respected and protected for their individual contribution to a balanced nature.

Alien plants

Have you ever used a flower guide to aid in identifying a wildflower and found after its name, "alien"? It is surprising, and fascinating too, to find that many wild flowering plants that we take for granted were not here at the time Columbus discovered America, but were introduced at a later time. Probably their American ancestry is no older than that of American families who came early to these shores to settle the land.

How these alien plants reached America undoubtedly would make romantic, almost unbelievable tales. There is a possibility that seeds were wafted for thousands of miles by winds to a strange, unexplored continent. Or, they may have been carelessly brought in ballast in stout sailing vessels bringing trade to our struggling colonies. The colonists themselves may have brought seeds from the gardens of their native lands across the Atlantic to plant around their new homes in the North American wilderness.

One of our showiest and most common wildflowers, one that flaunts its gaudy beauty along country roadsides in July, is the wild day lily, so called because its bloom lasts only a day. It has two interesting records hanging on its family tree: it is an alien and it is an escapee from cultivated gardens. Its place of origin is eastern Asia. Think how far this species has traveled to reach the inland states of a distant continent.

It should be a snobbish dowager, being a lily that is innately stately, but instead it is a friendly vagabond that lavishly broadcasts its tawny flowers across the land, even encroaching upon home gardens. (I have some in my yard that are double.)

Wherever you see this bright orange lily, you may be sure that two other alien wildflowers, the heavenly blue chicory and the pretty Queen Anne's lace, will be found close by. These three companionable plants make an attractive landscaping effect throughout July's hot, dry weather. Heat and drought have little adverse effect on them. They possess a kind of stamina that endears them to us when other flowers droop in the heat.

There never was a prettier blue than the blue that colors the chicory. It can't compare to the subtle, indescribable blue of the fringed gentian but it nevertheless is an honest lavender-blue that delights the eye. The blossom has many narrow rays, the tip of each being daintily fringed.

Chicory is a useful plant. Several varieties are planted for a specific purpose, one for its stout roots that are used as an adulterant for coffee. During the Civil War, it served as a coffee substitute. Some shoots are bleached for salads and one variety has tasty, tender leaves.

Queen Anne's lace, a lacy flat umbel of tiny florets, stands two to three feet tall. Its foliage is deeply cut, looking much like the leaf of the cultivated carrot in our vegetable gardens. In fact, the two plants are related and one of Queen Anne's lace's common names is "wild carrot." In the center of large umbels is a brownish-purple floret that looks like a raisin in a sugar cookie.

Queen Anne's lace is abundant and gives to the heavy, robust summer plants a lift of airy grace. It blooms over a long period of time — some of the late flowers are still attractive until early frosts.

Mature flowers gather the outer edges toward the center into a cup-like form that resembles a bird's nest, this protects the ripening seeds. In one umbel an observer once counted 782 seeds. These unique seed clusters have given this plant another common name, "bird's nest weed."

Mockingbird

A pole, telephone-pole size and height, stands in my neighbor's yard and bears the large arc light that illuminates their grounds and mine at night. It is flat on top and it is one of the busiest spots in the community, for a mockingbird has selected it for a resting spot, a lookout and a stage.

I said resting spot, but one wonders when this bundle of nervous energy ever rests. He flies upward from the distant fence row where his mate is evidently brooding her eggs and with a pretentious flexing of wings and spreading of tail he lands on the pole. He is no more than settled when he starts shuffling his feet about as if the surface on which he stands is hot. Then he bounds into the air, feet dangling, wings beating to keep him aloft, then down he comes.

His next excursion into the air might be a flip-flop, awkward and comic, as if every bone in his body had turned to rubber and he might come apart at any moment. All the time he's going through this performance he's "running off at the mouth" as country folk describe a too talkative person, screeching, scolding, chortling and sometimes singing.

What a gay, lunatic creature this mocker is! With all his carrying-on one doesn't miss the lack of other mid-summer bird music. He can run the gamut of other bird song, the raucous calls of crows, jays, crested flycatcher, killdeer, even cackling of hens out in the barnyard, to the soft notes of the robin and bluebird, cardinal and Carolina wren. Once or twice I've heard him repeat the whistle of the titmouse and experiment with the Baltimore oriole's song as it sang from the nearby maple.

Slowly the mockingbird has taken over the land. I saw my first mockingbird in Ohio in 1924 when I visited a farm on Liberty Road with a bird-watching friend.

Its appearance caused excitement among the small Audubon group of that period and I remember how proudly the farmer welcomed all who came to see the strange bird. Now the mocker is considered a common resident species.

The mockingbird is not entirely popular. He's arrogant and tyrannical, chasing small birds from winter feeding stations and establishing himself as lord of the manor. Some people object to his singing at night.

But he's a handsome fellow. His streamlined body, dressed in pearl gray with handsome white wing bars and saucy tail outlined in white feathers, is graceful and perfectly coordinated. His vitality, entertaining behavior and outstanding musical talents counteract any bad manners he might have and endear him to those who have the grace not to cast the first stone.

Sometimes when sleep fails and the nights are long, it is good to hear the mockingbird's clear sweet music ring out. Usually, but not always, the night is moonlit. Peace comes, the music grows softer, more tender. God's in his heaven, all's well with the world.

Barnswallows

Occasionally one might make a single unusual bird observation or have an outstanding experience that gives immediate pleasure that might be considered a bonus in the broad scope of bird watching. But to have continued intimate association with an individual bird species over a period of years might be regarded as unique.

For several years barnswallows have visited my garden. Why, I can't understand, for my lawn is long and narrow, edged with trees and shrubs and not large enough to provide the wide sweep of space barnswallows need for feeding.

They follow as the lawn is being mowed, swooping daintily and feeding as the insects are stirred up by the movement of the mower through the grass. They twitter as they effortlessly lift their almost weightless bodies, now low, then up, tree-high, then low again as they continue feeding.

They like to perch on the electric light wire that stretches from the house to the garage. This spot catches the first rays of the rising sun. Here they rest, preen their feathers, stretch and communicate with each other by twittering in a pleasant friendly fashion. They're active but not nervous. Their quick movement gives the impression of joy, happiness, perfect freedom without care.

For the past three years the old birds have brought their young here to bask in the early morning light where the sun beams down with concentrated heat. They also like to rest on the warm roof of the garage, wings expanded, twittering their food call which the old birds answer with quick concern.

Today the old birds paid their respects and presented their young for my approval. They staged a showy mass flight over the garden. Tree-top high, all the birds, seven in number, flew close together, sweeping, turning, soaring, constantly twittering as if they had some message to deliver. Suddenly they wheeled and alighted in the topmost branches of a tall spruce. Only a brief rest was necessary, then they were up and away.

It is impossible to describe adequately the beauty, the grace, the joy of living these birds impart to the human observers whose hearts and minds are receptive to their charm.

I've never located the nest of these barnswallows. Long ago barns disappeared from this neighborhood and I presume the birds plaster their pretty clay-mud nests to some building. In southern Ohio, where they are common, barnswallows' nests are frequently found on outer walls of dwellings.

I trust I can regard all birds objectively, that I am not guilty of attributing to them anthropomorphic qualities they do not possess. That could brand me as an incompetent observer and reporter. But it is difficult for me to look on "my" barnswallows as automatons without a degree of intelligence and purpose.

M   E   R

Flowers of summer

These are the golden days, gold edging to orange and paling to yellow. No matter what the tone, the effect is golden.

Butterfly weed sends up golden flares in sun-drenched fields. This plant is libelously misnamed. Never throughout its range does it reach an abundance that would make it troublesome to agriculture, so it never attains characteristics that would brand it a weed. Weed it is not, but one of the glorious wild plants of midsummer. Sometimes a delicate yellow butterfly weed is found.

The blooms of this plant attract a multitude of insect guests to their sweet nectar. Butterflies, of course, else why the name? But bees of all species, brilliant small beetles, tiny flies and wasps linger long at their bounty. And when the flowers are spent they leave the prettiest tiny seed pods that can be found in all outdoors.

Butterfly weed has companions in the same color range that make the meadows and country roadsides a joy to behold. Black-eyed susans grow near their smaller relatives, the thin-leaved coneflower. In the Dayton area the small coneflower is more abundant and is often erroneously identified as black-eyed susan.

As you wend your way southward, the larger flower becomes more predominant and is one of our most robust wildflowers. It is remarkable how long these plants remain fresh in the heat of summer.

Along country roads where spraying and mowing have not taken their toll the tall tawny day lily lifts its orange cup to the sun. This plant grows naturally in masses and its brilliant flowers catch and hold the sun's power and brightness with stunning effect.

There are other yellow-gold flowers in bloom, Jerusalem artichoke, green-headed coneflower, several species of wild sunflower, evening primrose and many more.

Gold sets the scene. It is the time of relentless heat of the summer sun and flowers revel in the warmth, the color, the glow that comes from the blazing star that gives them life.

But all sun and no contrast could be overpowering, suffocating, so nature, wise gardener that she is, causes flowers of contrasting shades to tone down the fiery heat of gold. Dainty Queen Anne's lace sends up her frilly whiteness beside the day lily's bright glow and not far off the cool heavenly blue of the chicory is like a drink of cold water to a traveler in the desert.

Farther south the exquisite flowering spurge adds a cooling effect to "hot" flowers. Out in the field near the butterfly weed, the ox-eye daisy, the most faithful of all wild flowers, stands by. This indefatigable wildling blooms from May through August, the white rays cool, but its round yellow center pays tribute to the sun.

Bouncing Bet

Bouncing Bet is a flower traveler of distinction. Her distinction doesn't stem from beauty or grace, for she's a stout, buxom plebian, but from her staunch stamina that led her, an escapee from European gardens, across the ocean to a new land.

Not content to stay placidly at home in colonial New England gardens, she started to explore New York on her own and now she's traveled the breadth and length of our land.

Bouncing Bet isn't fastidious about choosing a place to take root. Roadsides are her favorite location and that's where she's most often seen. In the days when traveling on the railroad was the commonest mode of transportation, we found her growing along the tracks. She won't shun an unsightly dump and I once saw a beautiful bed of the indiscriminate Bets growing out of a slag pile near a coal mine in West Virginia.

Bouncing Bet is pink and not a pretty pink at that. When you come to think about it, I don't recall another pink flower comparable to it. Most pinks are rosy, or verging to a deep rose, lavender rose, or magenta. Bouncing Bet's pink is pale and insipid.

But the lass has a sturdy persistence that commands respect. Among common names given this plant whose botanical name is *saponaria officinalis*, we find Soapwort, Soapwort Gentian, Scourwort, and the references to cleansing propensities are well-founded. Bruised stems, leaves and roots, when stirred around in water, will make suds.

In pioneer days Bouncing Bet laid some claim to medicinal virtues. That was why colonial housewives planted it in dooryard gardens. It was asserted that "a decoction of leaves will cure the itch" and it was used in long gone days as a remedy for venereal disease. Herbals, however, warn that Bouncing Bet should be used with care, intimating that the remedy might be worse then the disease.

It's interesting to glance through old botanies and books on weeds and herbs and note how many "worts" there are. "Wort" is an ancient word for root and the Anglo-Saxon word "wyrt" means herb.

In the early settlement of our country, doctors were scarce and those who practiced their profession were not well trained. "Yarbs" (herbs) had an important place in supplying home remedies for common ailments. What a revelation of needs and their easement the colloquial names tell: soapwort, a substitute for soap; toothwort; sneezewort; wartwort. Gutwort certainly is not an elegant name, but who cared about that if it helped a stomachache, or should one be consistent and say bellyache?

Worts, their name is legion, about 150 species, and all are named appropriately, indicating the cure for the ailment man is heir to.

Nature's constancy

I always have a drastic reaction when I hear someone on a television talk show or in a private conversation glibly say, "I don't believe in God," or "There is no God." I've heard it said so often I shouldn't be affected by it, but I am. It gives me a queer "gone" feeling. How could one be so arrogant, flip?

Those who enjoy a close kinship with nature — particularly those who live where there is a change of seasons and experience the exhilaration of the renewal of life in spring, the seedtime of summer, the harvest of autumn, the restorative process of the rest of winter — learn firsthand the infinite power of the Creator, the inexorable operation of his laws that control the universe without caprice or error. None of our prayers could change or sway it in any way. How awesome this knowledge is, yet how comforting.

But it is not the awesome power, the might of God that attract us most. It is the constancy, the dependability, the smooth, ordered operation of natural forces that we can grasp with our finite minds and emotions that draw us to belief. We go to sleep untroubled about morning light breaking, for it always does. We take for granted the miracle of rain and think about it selfishly only when it rains too much, spoils a picnic or doesn't rain for weeks.

How can we be stirred by the majesty of a snow-capped mountain touching the clouds without being aware of its Creator? How much more deeply touched are we by the sweet perfection of the tiny spring beauty, a simple little flower, yet exquisite in its coloring, inspiring in its courage, stamina and will to survive. The lofty mountain and the wee flower show the Creator working in magnitude and in miniature.

The constancy of nature to those aware of its timing brings peace of mind and is also a source of anticipation: We know what event is coming, but it never palls, never grows stale or boring. We can almost set the date for the spring arrival of the first chimney swift, Baltimore oriole or chipping sparrow.

The chitter of the swifts overhead is the most cheerful sound of summer, and to watch their erratic dash across the sky is one of life's simple pleasures. The flash of the oriole's oriental splendor across May's blue heaven is priceless, yet it is a free gift from a benevolent Creator. When you run down the chipping sparrow's tuneless song, you find the cunningest, perkiest little bird imaginable, who likes humans so well he'll place his trim, rounded nest in the evergreen at the kitchen door.

In July comes the dependable recurrence of a triumvirate of wild flowers you can't miss.

They are the tawny day lily, burning orange red; the chicory, colored a blue worked out on the Creator's easel so cunningly that it cannot be described or duplicated; and the white froth of Queen Anne's lace worthy of a queen, yet its daintiness is not delicate but has the stout substance fit for a plebian's lean pocketbook.

Lilies are not always the chaste white flowers found on the altar on Easter morn. Many are opulent, of robust color and do much to animate our gardens. But our tawny wild day lily is a tramp with a flair. It scorns the haughty, well-planned garden of the affluent and brightens the highways of life. It waves a gay hand in greeting to all who pass along its way.

And it hobnobs with the chicory, knowing that its blue is a perfect foil for the lily's bright hue, and the Queen Anne's lace that wears a coarse, common replica of a queen's fine lace. Truly, God's in His Heaven and He's doing right well with His world.

S   U   M

Bald eagle

He clasps the crag with crooked hands
Close to the sun in lonely lands
Ring'd with the azure world he stands.
— Tennyson

Whether he soars the azure world or rests on some mighty crag, the American bald eagle stuns you by his enormous dignity, his strength, his power. That he represents our country as our national emblem adds significance to his status. Our hearts beat faster at the sight of this symbolic bird.

He did not, however, attain his exalted place in the symbolism that surrounds the bird, the flag, the shield of our land without opposition. In a speech to the young Congress meeting in Philadelphia in 1782, Benjamin Franklin said:

"For my part, I wish the bald eagle had not been chosen as the representative of our country; he is a bird of bad moral character. In truth, the (wild turkey) is, in comparison, a much more respectable bird and withall a true original native of America. Eagles have been found in all countries, but the turkey is peculiar to ours. He is besides (though a little vain and silly, it is true, but not a worse emblem for that) a bird of courage and would not hesitate to attack a grenadier of the British guard who should presume to invade his farmyard with a red coat on."

For once the wise doctor was overruled and the bald eagle became our national emblem.

What characteristics did our bald eagle possess that led Franklin to brand him a creature of "bad moral character?" He is accused of two sins — laziness and thievery. He and another bird of prey, the fishhawk or osprey, are found in the same areas. Both birds are fond of fish, which makes up a large percentage of their diet.

The bald eagle will hunt fish if he has to, but before he'll work for his food, he'll eat dead fish that are available along shore, or will rob an osprey of a catch he worked honestly to obtain. The osprey will eat a dead fish if it is fresh, but will not eat carrion.

The eagle hunts crows, waterfowl, small mammals — most rodents — for himself and for his young. He spends much of his time sitting on some favorite perch and moves only if motivated by hunger or excited by the appearance of game or the approach of man. Nothing escapes his phenomenal eyesight.

Most authorities who have studied our national bird have concluded he is an errant coward. He often is caught without defending himself and when trapped he is docile, allowing handling without hostility or attempting to escape. But there are enough belligerent individuals among bald eagles to prove the exception to the rule.

When eagles are attacked by smaller birds, particularly the crow, they look on the lesser bird with dignified indifference. Crows love to pester eagles, but sometimes the tables are turned. An observer once watched a crow fly down and peck an eagle repeatedly; then, growing bolder, alight on its back and peck its head. Whereupon the eagle plummeted headlong into deep water, carrying the crow with it.

Eagles build large, deep, strong nests that are used year after year. The most famous of all eagle nests was the Great Nest built in a shell bark hickory tree in Vermillion, Ohio, not later than 1890. It was added to and occupied every year thereafter until blown down in a storm in 1925.

Burroughs once said of the bald eagle: "Dignity, elevation and repose are his. I would have my thoughts take as wide a sweep. I would be as far removed from the petty cares and turmoils of this noisy and blustering world."

M   E   R

Spiders

Do you remember the Greek myth that relates the weaving contest between Athena, goddess of the air, and a young maiden, Arachne, who was a skilled spinner and weaver and boasted that she owed her skill to no one, not even Athena?

Of course Athena won the contest. As a punishment for Arachne's presumption in challenging a goddess, Athena turned her into a spider so that she could continue her talent in another form.

Spiders have, therefore, been given the scientific classification Arachnida, invertebrate animals having two body sections, four pairs of jointed legs and no antennae or wings.

We are now entering that time of year when we are very conscious of spiders. The housewife feels their clinging web across her face as she walks down the basement stairs. She finds their festoons in corners and on walls, in the living quarters of her home, and she arms herself with cleaning tools to rid her household of these unwelcome guests.

We do not escape them outdoors, either. We feel the same invisible threads of silk in the face as we walk across an open field in the bright sunshine, but seldom see the wee traveler that floats along on his silken transportation.

The dew-drenched vegetation on an early morning walk reveals all manner of webs made by the descendants of the chastised Arachne who dared to affront the goddess of the air.

Spiders are unique for their ability to weave with silk. Some insects in their caterpillar stage spin silk to line their cocoons for protection of their immature form during metamorphosis. But spider's silk is pure protein and its production drains both energy and protein from the spider's body. They can only be replaced by the spider being able to capture food that is entrapped in the sticky portion of the web. If it is not able to catch food it will eat some dispensable part of its web.

Most of us are familiar with the large circular orb webs spun by garden spiders. They are spun with the skill of a master engineer. Drag or guy lines fastened to vegetation at intervals not only anchor the web securely, but also act as safety routes. Spiders retrace their paths on these lines and they serve as delicate communication devices telling the vigilant spider of an intrusion on its web.

Most of the spider web structure is of dry silk. The coarse spiral lines running down the center of the orb are strands of sticky

thread called catching spiral.

Except for man, the caddis fly and fungus gnats, spiders are the only animals that make traps to catch their food. Spider silk looks like the most fragile thing in nature but it has great strength and elasticity, and is expressly adapted for holding or enveloping a struggling victim. Even so, some insects might escape, but the spider, a prisoner destined to live in the confines of the prison it built for itself, dashes in for a quick bite or a paralyzing sting.

There are many different types of spider webs. Along with the handsome orb web there are funnel webs, air dome webs, underground webs lined with silk, trap door webs, webs made of masses of criss-cross silken threads. Some spiders do not build webs at all but make retreats under rocks or logs or bark of trees.

Jumping spiders build permanent webs only when the female deposits her eggs. The tiny crab spider hides in flowers to catch the small insects that are attracted to the blossoms. It camouflages its presence by taking on the color of the flower.

The small ballooning spiders are renowned travelers. The little fellow climbs up a tall blade of grass and awaits a breeze of some velocity. He then spreads his legs, tilts up his abdomen and slowly plays out a long strand of silk. The breeze makes him airborne and off he goes. Darwin found a ballooning spider on his boat 60 miles off shore, but since that time they have been found 200 miles out at sea and 10,000 feet in altitude.

The spinning organs are glands that produce different types of silk, dry silk, sticky elastic silk, coarse threads that are adhesive. They lead to two or three pairs of spinnerets on the abdomen and are finger-like in form. At the end of each spinneret there are many tiny tubes from which the silk is spun.

There are 30,000 known spiders in our world, and it is believed that that number is only one-fourth of the total.

Spiders have been studied by many outstanding naturalists and their published works make good reading. They've found that spiders' feeding habits benefit man by destroying many species of noxious insects. They realize that spiders are feared and misunderstood through prejudice and lack of knowledge of their habits. They learned that the bite of the common spider is not dangerous. The hard-working spider deserves the respect and admiration of the human sojourner on this planet, earth.

M   E   R

Thistle

Several years ago I found an attractive rosette of basal leaves of a plant growing in the lawn near my house. The leaves were long, narrow and sharply pointed with a prominent midrib. The soft gray-green leaves shown as if they had been waxed and polished but there the softness ended for the edges of the leaves were armed with sharp stout spines as formidable as any I'd ever seen on a local plant.

I knew at once it was a thistle, but it was unlike any thistle I knew.

Since I couldn't identify it, I decided to let it grow, knowing that I could use the tools of my trade eventually to identify the mature plant.

And grow it did — into one of the handsomest gray-green stalks of miniature stilettoes of leaves that ever grew. There was no way of touching the plant anywhere without drawing blood. Each drooping stem bore a large pompom of bloom. This drooping stem, bent at the base of the flower, identified the plant immediately as the nodding thistle.

The flower is rich reddish purple and the bracts, sharply pointed and recurved, are deep purple. Prickly wings spread along the stalk, adding to its bristling appearance. The entire plant shouts, "Don't touch me!" yet the drooping head is demure and shyly extends a warm welcome to every passing bee.

It stood dignified in its royal purple, four feet in height. It was stunning, by far the

most outstanding flower in my garden. But I live in a semi-rural community and certainly I didn't want to be guilty of causing the spread of a plant that might be troublesome to crops or difficult to control. My sense of civic responsibility led me to practice birth control. As each flower head turned gray with ripening seeds I cut it off and burned it.

Nevertheless, each spring a few of the rosettes come up in the yard. Reluctantly, I'd dig them up. This year, however, my garden was such a disaster from the effects of the long, cold winter and the audacious late freeze in April that I didn't have the heart to destroy a handsome plant of the nodding thistle that appeared in the lawn.

Due to the lack of rain and intense heat it didn't grow as tall as usual, but the flowers are gorgeous. It alone had the stamina to survive the heat and drought, so I salute it. When the flowers are spent I cut them off so the seeds won't go gallivanting off on some giddy breeze and settle in some farmer's soybean field.

Perhaps there are other nodding thistles nearby but mine is the only one I know about. The closest I've seen them is along a country road in Clark County leading to Cedar Bog.

Most of the thistles found in our valley are aliens. Native of Mediterranean Eurasia and northern Africa, they are handsome plants but are branded as weeds in America. The edges of their leaves are deeply notched and bristled. The spines protect the plants. They are a defense against animal intrusion but insects are drawn to the tubular flowers as by a magnet.

The pasture or bull thistle is one of the beauties of late summer and early autumn. Being a familiar, common flower does not degrade its charm. The silvery gray cast to its green foliage accents the lavender of the flower, and if it grows near goldenrod and the royal purple of the ironweed, the simple roadside scene they create gives it an honored place on lists of American heritage.

Interestingly enough our native thistles have yellow flowers, flat as those of the dandelion. They are handsome and prickly but not so showy or stalwart as the aliens. Their names are unimaginative, too — field sow thistle, common sow thistle and spiny-leaved sow thistle.

Like most families, either plant or animal, thistles have a black sheep, and the Canada thistle is theirs. This species grows in a cool climate, from Canada southward, our valley being the limit of its southern distribution.

Canada thistles have small pale lavender flowers, and narrow leaves, slightly prickly. It is sometimes called the "creeping thistle" a name that suits it well as it sends new plants up from long creeping roots that extend far from the parent plant. It is hard to control, a nuisance, and presents a serious problem to our local agriculture.

M   E   R

Weeds

I have always had a profound respect for weeds. Long before I understood what an important role they play in our natural world I regarded them emotionally.

One of the earliest tasks assigned me as a child was to pull weeds from our vegetable garden. Since there were scores of things I'd rather do, I looked on weed-pulling with hate and resentment that weeds grew where food plants were supposed to grow and self-pity that I was elected to work their extermination.

Later on as I learned them by name I reacted emotionally to their beauty, to finding them in some unexpected place in a setting that was pleasing. An English naturalist once said, "I do not want change, I want the same wildflowers, the same song birds singing . . . and I want them in the same place."

And so, seeing moneywort's golden coins glowing in the meadow grass, wild mustard blooming yellow in the field, lacy white water hemlock in some moist place along the highway, the oxeye daisy lifting its innocent face to the sun, chicory and Queen Anne's lace and day lily complementing each other along the roadside in midsummer heat, followed by goldenrod, thistle and ironweed in the fields and the snowy snake root, ghostlike in the woods year after year, satisfied my love of beauty and gave me a sense of security in Nature's consistent continuity. The same loved things in the same place at the same time.

As time passed, my respect for weeds took on deeper significance. For I appreciated their "supervitality," which makes possible their survival through all kinds of adverse growing conditions and change made by man's use and management of the land. When man relaxes his vigilance in the never-ending task of cultivation, weeds take over, holding in place the soil and using their potential for improving it.

One is impressed by the ancient interdependence between man and weeds, those plants that grow where we want something else to grow. Weeds were the mother of medicine, for early in the history of the races of man they learned the healing properties of many weeds. Many were and still are used for food.

Weed control in our food and flower gardens is of general concern. I control weeds on my place by pulling them up. Some weeds are a trial and an abomination. I have an unending struggle with grass, quack, crab, foxtail, etc. Bindweed and sand weed are two persistent vines, hard to control.

Out in the lawn, gill-over-the-ground, a creeping weed and unwelcome intruder from England, is another pest hard to control. Broad leaf plantain and buckhorn are persistent but not too difficult to manage. There are other weeds, too, many others.

But there is one dainty little weed that I don't like to disturb and I always leave a plant or two for my own pleasure. My grandmother called it "sweet fern" and I had a time to find its botanical name. With the help of friends I found it to be *artemesia annua*.

I love its dainty foliage, but most of all I revel in its sweet fragrance that perfumes the area where other rank smelling weeds grow.

S　　　　　　U　　　　　　M

July

Sharp as a sickle is the edge of shade and shine. Earth in her heart laughs, looking at the heavens. Thinking of the harvest, I look and think of mine.

— Meredith

July is a plump matron gathering her crops. She is sun-bronzed and the deep blue of her eyes shows faintly gray from looking at the sun. July is opulent, sated with fruit of May's planting.

July is practical, for hers is the harvest of April's tender showers; May's warm, pregnant soil; June's long perfection of sun and rain, earth and sky.

July offers at her altar the first sweet corn, green beans, squash, luscious melons and the first fruits of the orchard.

July wears a finished look — the finished bird's nest worn down by the restlessness of fledglings; the finished brood itself now on the wing. The fresh, perfect night moths, the butterflies released to light from dark confines of cocoon and chrysalis. March lambs, now staid from their playful gamboling, young colts showing off in green pastures, young calves being primed for the market, the second or third generation of young rabbits nibbling at late gardens.

July brings strangulating heat, and her nights do not bring relief. But it takes long days and nights of heat for harvests to mature, and it falls on July to do the job.

There is a dry dustiness to July, a hint of aging. Foliage everywhere lacks the spit and polish of May and June. Grass on lawns has lost its Irish green, the fields take on the tans and browns of harvested crops. The long graceful blades of corn still wave green, but basal leaves grow sere.

Young birds of the season start wandering in July. The young of starlings, grackles and redwings fly about the country in small family groups. Starlings are a dull ugly brown and grackles' plumage lacks brilliance. As they journey, their squawks and calls sound much like the food calls they made while being fed in the nest. All this behavior is preparatory to building up the vast flocks that take off in migratory flight later on.

July brings strong scents and tastes. Mint is at its height in July. It is a large family and many species are used in cooking, for flavor in food and drink. It gives off pleasant spicy fragrances when trod underfoot or crushed in the hand — spearmint, peppermint, pennyroyal and bergamot, to name a few. Their pungent odors only increase and complement the sweetness of honeysuckle and clover.

Many of July's flowers are large, heavy, coarse. Take the elderberry that produces large, heavy umbels composed of countless tiny florets, each in itself a perfect flower. Queen Anne's lace produces similar growth, as do the yarrow and wild water hemlock.

Hal Borland referred to these composites as each being a "flower city," suggesting that flowers, as well as man, are gregarious and like living close together.

M   E   R

August nights

August's "nights have a thousand eyes," all outshone by the round orb of the moon. How placidly it rides across the sable sky, controlled, remotely cool, but never cold or forbidding.

August's nights have a thousand sounds, busy, shrill, offbeat and low hums that actually are buzzes requiring a trained ear to detect the difference.

August's nocturnal concerts are by small insects, minnesingers that, lacking the vocal equipment of birds, compensate by dominating the night.

The air pulsates with sound. There must be millions of unseen performers that set the dark wood and sleeping fields vibrating with the volume of their music. Yet, only three species — the coneheaded grasshoppers, katydids and crickets — really "sing." The music is produced by rubbing together their wings, a membranous framework with thickened ridges, or veins. The songs all vary in cadence, tempo, tonal quality and volume, and each species can be identified by its song. Only the males sing.

Crickets are merry little musicians. Most everyone knows the lively little brown field cricket that sometimes gets into our houses and keeps us awake by singing his shrill song. He is not welcome on our hearth, but outside he really bears the burden of song in the great chorus where his talent is appreciated.

The snowy tree cricket sings from the trees. It is pale green, sometimes white and perhaps is the most accomplished of all the nocturnal musical group. These crickets are gregarious and apparently enjoy banding together in certain areas and singing throughout the night. There is a fine congregation of them on our hilltop, but recently I spent the evening in the garden of a friend south of Dayton and did not hear the snowy cricket there.

The snowy cricket is a willing weather helper, for, if you know his secret, he will give you the temperature of your immediate vicinity. Count the number of chirps he utters in 15 seconds, add 40, and the sum will be the degree of temperature. It is fairly accurate, seldom varying more than one or two degrees.

The very modest little bush cricket, brown with a yellow parallel stripe on its side, sings a minor, low-beat song down in the shrubbery. One cannot tell if it is a hum or a buzz.

Many people are conscious of the katydid's emphatic song. Katy is a pretty green insect easily found, but it is often confused with the coneheaded grasshopper, which is also green and about the same size. However, the katydid sings from the trees and the coneheaded grasshopper seeks tall grass and weeds for singing posts.

Sometimes the cicada extends its singing into the night, but it is considered diurnal.

Insects' serenades reach a crescendo in late August that continues into early September. Slowly, the volume subsides until it is entirely stopped by frost. While it lasts, the unique music adds to the interest of the night, accenting its beauty, its moods, its sounds, its mystery.

S   U   M

Pokeweed

Now is the time for our largest weed to come into its own. I hesitate to use the term weed when discussing this plant because of the unpopularity of weeds. Since this so-called weed, the pokeweed, is one of my favorite things, I'd like others to look on it with admiration and pleasure, too.

A mature, full grown pokeweed is something to behold, especially if it grows alone without being crowded by competing plants. Its size is most impressive and commands the attention of the most casual observer. Botany reference books say it sometimes reaches a height of eight feet, but for years a pokeweed that was 10 to 12 feet tall grew in my garden. Unfortunately it did not survive the effects of last winter's severe temperatures.

Pokeweed is a perennial plant. In its development during the growing season it reaches the size of a small tree. The stems are large and hollow and are many branched, the leaves are large and pointed, and are a lively green with stems that are purplish red. The entire plant has a gracefully spreading shape.

The poke blossom is a raceme of pretty, off-white florets that produce chartreuse berries that ripen to a rich, deep purple. The tiny stems of florets and berries are reddish. In late August, racemes of florets, green berries and ripe berries all appear at the same time giving the plant a vigorous, varied attractiveness, a robust good looks that should make it welcome in the most sophisticated garden.

Thoreau described the pokeberry as "all afire with ripeness." Other naturalists, who write interestingly of the poke for the layman and do not confuse him with unpronounceable scientific names, have given this largest of all our herbs at least 15 common names, one of which is most appropriate, inkberry. The early settlers used its purple-red juice for ink and to give it the colloquial name "inkberry" was logical.

Pokeweed is a contradictory plant. Its roots and ripe berries are poisonous, but the leaves make a delicious early spring greens dish. The first spring shoots may be boiled and eaten like asparagus. I confess I have to take the word of hardy souls who have eaten pokeweed with enthusiasm, as to its tastiness and safety as human food, for I've never been brave enough to try it myself.

Pokeberry is a medicinal herb. A drug, the tincture of phytolacca (the scientific name for pokeweed) is extracted from the dried berries and roots of the plant. When it is mixed with lanolin, farmers use it to cure swelling and caking of cows' udders.

Pokeweed is a widely used food resource for wildlife, too. Twenty-five species of birds eat the ripe berries, but the mockers and thrushes feed most heavily on the fruit. Robins particularly are responsible for distributing the seeds in their droppings which will start growing in any rich, moist soil. The red and the gray foxes, opossum, raccoon and the wee white-footed mouse relish the ripe, juicy berries. Pokeweed is easily controlled.

This fine plant grows across the entire eastern half of our country, from the Atlantic coast to the foothills of the Rockies, from Canada to the Gulf States. Its striking good looks, its usefulness as food, its limited medicinal use, make it a respected part of the flora of our land. Its adaptability to any terrain, any kind of weather, sunshine or semi-shade, shows how well it accommodates itself to its environment.

M   E   R

Bats

The little bat that you might have observed flittering across the sky at dusk on late summer evenings is the strangest of all animals. It is a true mammal, that is, it is born alive from its mother's body; it is fed on mammary glands; its body is covered with hair or fur and it has four legs.

In the bat the two front legs have been modified for flight which gives it habits common with birds. But the bat cannot be regarded even as a link between these two orders of animals.

Bats are so unique and the order to which they belong is so sharply defined that they do not encroach on any other order of mammals. They aren't remotely like any other living creature. There are two orders of bats, the fruit-eating bats found only in the Old World and the small insect-eating bats that are found in nearly every land. These are the bats that are indigenous to North America.

Bats are creatures of the night. For this reason many of their habits are not understood, in fact they have not as yet been studied. This is why an aura of mystery and ghoulish legends about them have grown out of ignorance and fear.

The bones of the arms and fingers are fantastically elongated and across this bony framework a thin membrane is stretched. It reaches from the bat's side to the fingertips, to the ankle joints of the hind legs and from there to the tip of the tail, thus enclosing most of the body in membraneous tissues. At the front angle of the wing is a tiny thumb bearing a claw.

I once asked a class of kindergartners, "Why do you think Mother Nature put a thumb on the little bat's wing?" I received a most erudite answer from one wee one who said "Tho he could thuck it!"

The wings close up snugly against the bat's body like an umbrella and the thumbs help the bat to crawl over a flat surface. It also uses the thumb to scratch the back of its head and to help smooth its fur when it grooms itself.

The membrane in the wings has a network of highly sensitized nerves which warn the bat of any obstacle in its flight.

Bats' ears are erect and fairly large in proportion to the size of the body. Their hearing operates like a radar system, is phenomenally keen, and picks up sounds the human ear is incapable of hearing.

For countless generations the bat has been the victim of ignorance, prejudice and old wives' tales, all of which have built up unfounded fears in minds of people who have believed the stories without taking the pains either to corroborate or expose them as false.

One of the commonest accusations against the bat is that it likes to become entangled in women's hair. Nonsense! Such a situation would cause the bat more consternation than the woman would suffer. Moreover, the bat's built-in physical alarm systems would prevent such an event happening.

In a laboratory test a blinded bat was once released in a room that was criss-crossed with threads. It flew about and never became entangled. This acute hearing, along with the sensitive nervous system in the wing membrane, makes it possible for the bat to fly with terrific speed through trees and never strike a twig. It would instinctively avoid entanglement in women's tresses.

The belief that the bat is dirty and carries vermin is pure slander. Lice, never

S U M

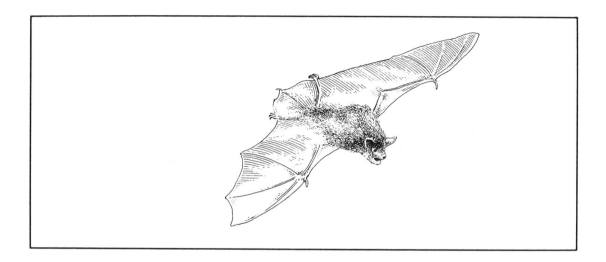

communicable to man, have been found on bats, but normally they are the cleanest animals in the world, and are very particular about their personal hygiene.

With the adaptable claw on his thumb the bat scratches then smooths the fur, fine as silk, on head and back, then licks the claw clean. Like a cat he licks the underparts of his body. He washes his face with the tip of his wing, then licks the wing clean.

The way he stretches, pulls and tugs at his wings as he licks them meticulously is wonderful to behold. It's a good thing they are elastic or they could not withstand the rough treatment they get. His tiny feet are also useful in scratching surfaces his thumb cannot reach. This grooming takes many minutes out of his busy day.

An almost universal belief that bats are vampires and will attack humans and domestic animals is a gross misconception of the true worth of our little brown bat. True, there are vampire bats in South America but there is none in the United States.

Bats feed on aerial insects, mainly gnats and mosquitoes, but other flying insects, beetles, dragonflies, etc., have been found in their stomach contents. They are caught in the apron or cup the bat makes out of his flexible tail. He bends over, scoops them into his mouth and chews them with his fine sharp teeth as any other mammal, including you and I, disposes of its food.

Some bats migrate but many hibernate in winter, hanging head down and clinging to the walls of caves, hollow trees, outbuildings or even in the garrets of dwelling houses. They are almost in a comatose state with respiration extremely low. Once we had several bats hibernate in the cold cellar in our greenhouse.

There they rest until the warmth of spring starts insect movement and the little bat wakens to start his important work anew.

Hawks

Watching the matchless soaring of turkey vultures and the wheeling and turning of the red-shouldered hawks high in the sky above Adams County's wooded hills caused me to ponder the history and present status of these fine birds of prey.

Two vultures, the turkey and the black vulture, are both recorded in this county, yet on frequent visits and one six-week's stay in the area I never once observed the black species. Turkey vultures are numerous. Almost any time of day after air currents and thermal drafts are created by summer heat, you see them drifting across the heavens.

Two handsome species of buteo, the red shouldered and red-tailed hawks, are common but not abundant here. Time was when hawks were highly regarded by the rulers and nobility of lands of Europe and Asia and ancient Egypt. King Solomon, respected throughout the ages for his learning, once said that among the many things too wonderful for man to comprehend was "the way of an eagle in the air."

Hawks were considered with special regard by the nobility, for they were trained for use in the sport of kings, falconry. Each species had its rank: Peregrine, Goshawk and Gerfalcon for princes of the realm; Cooper's and Sharp-shinned for those of lower rank.

Imperial Rome set the eagle on the standards borne by its legions in all the lands it conquered. The helmets of brave Vikings were adorned with hawks' wings. On the American continent the proud red man sought perfect feathers from eagles and hawks for his war bonnet.

In spite of such honors, birds of prey have not fared well with man in modern times. Men with guns have come to regard birds with hooked beaks and curved talons as competitors, not fellow hunters. It is difficult to understand the logic that considers it "vicious" for a hawk or owl to kill a rabbit but an act of rugged sportsmanship when it is done by man. The bird is branded "vermin" even though most species seldom interfere with the quail and pheasant in the field, the fish in streams, the ducks and geese on ponds and lakes.

It has taken many years of professional wildlife research to change the attitude of hunters and farmers toward the birds of prey. The outstanding research of Dr. A. K. Fisher of the Department of Agriculture proved that the rodent control in the feeding of the great majority of hawks and owls entitled them to protection.

Continued study goes far beyond the importance of the economic service these birds render agriculture. Their place in the ecological balance of nature cannot be adequately estimated. They aid in population control; they feed on game and small birds that are ill, old and incapable of making a quick get-away, thus assuring a survival of the fittest.

Through enlightened study and more complete understanding we know that there are no "good" or "bad" birds. Each species is evolved to an instinctive pattern of behavior that indicates the kind of food it eats and governs the manner in which it is obtained.

S U M

Wrens

Wrens make up a most appealing family of birds. They're all good-looking, have interesting habits and most of them are accomplished singers.

Wrens' coloring runs to browns and tones of brown, distributed artistically so that they are not just any old common brown bird. Most wrens have short stiff tails held erect and, across the tails and extending down their rear ends, are chic horizontal bars of brown. With the exception of the house wren, the wrens in the Miami Valley have white eyelines that add interest and a certain air of smartness to their good looks.

Wrens are lively creatures, always on the go, but I never think of them as nervous or fidgety. They are curious, exploring every nook and cranny for food and examining any available place that might strike their fancy for nesting. Often the little fellow will halt his business and burst into song, and this is when his stance changes, for as he sings his tail droops. It's strange to associate the sagging tail with his merry outpouring of joyous music.

Locally the house wren and the Carolina wren are the species with which observers are most familiar. But an uncommon wren, the Bewick's (pronounced Buick as in car) is found here and nests sporadically.

It is really a choice bird, a maverick among the wrens. Its back is unstreaked charcoal brown, its breast clear white and its tail, as long as its body, is graceful and mobile as the bird twitches it frequently and often spreads it like a fan. The tail is prettily edged in off-white. This wren's song is especially lovely, as it is rendered "with a delicate air."

The last authentic nesting record I have for the Bewick's wren is 1969 when it nested successfully in a friend's garage in Shiloh.

A highly unusual nesting, however, occurred this summer in Springfield, Ohio, and the observer kept me up-to-date on the event.

A pair of Bewicks nested on the track of the garage door. The folks were pleased and didn't use the garage so the birds were not disturbed. Then came vacation time. The family was leaving town and felt that their garage should be closed and locked during their absence. The nest was completed and six eggs laid. What should be done?

Tests have proved that a nesting is often deserted if the nest is moved even a few inches to the right or left of the original position. The psychology of flight approach to the nest is involved. When I was consulted about moving the nest I was not very optimistic about the results, but there was no alternative. So it was placed in a shallow box and nailed to the wall about two inches above the exact position on the track. A pane from the window was removed for the birds to enter and leave the garage.

When the family returned home they were greeted with great excitement by the old birds who were feeding four fledglings. This is a success story and a happy one, for it is wonderful to have the tribe of this uncommon bird increase.

M   E   R

Hummingbird

I watched the incredible little bird poise as light as air above the columbine, dip its long beak into the flower and effortlessly pass on to another and another, its wings moving so rapidly they appeared as misty as the spray from the hose nearby.

Then, like a shot, it was gone. Later it perched on a dead twig on the hop hornbeam, rested, preened its feathers and then careened off into space.

Of course such behavior can be attributed to only one bird, the hummingbird, for no other bird is so tiny, so swift, or so capable of feeding on the wing, poised above its source of food with such absolute balance, power and grace.

Our little ruby-throated hummingbird is unique not only for its anatomical structure, beauty and interesting habits, but also for its distinction of being the only hummer east of the Rocky Mountains.

How lovely this wee creature is! Its feathers are metallic green on back, head and wings and the underparts are soft off-white. The male's throat is vivid ruby red. These birds need the refraction of the sun's rays to show up the rare brilliance and beauty of their coloring. No stuffed specimen can approximate the glowing fire of the ruby throat and the bright bronze shimmer of the green body feathers. The female's tail is rounded and daintily tipped with white, while the male's tail is perfectly straight across. The hummer looks more like a jewel than a bird.

The western hemisphere claims the hummingbird for its own, for it is not found in the Old World. There are 750 species and sub-species of hummingbirds with vast differences in color, size and manner of feeding, but all have their kind of flight in common. It is different from that of any other bird, as it moves so rapidly, its wings whir and its body seems like solid substance moving in a mist. The wings make 55 completed strokes a second while hovering; 61 a second while moving backward, and 75 a second when moving straight ahead.

The hummingbird looks so fragile one might think it would be shattered in rough weather, but it is tough. It flies the 500 miles across the Gulf of Mexico to its winter quarters in Central America non-stop.

This tiny mite has an irascible disposition. In fact, his beauty hides a fiery temper and his irritability is reflected in his sharp, complaining and sometimes whining calls that pass for a song. His temper is sharp and uncontrolled.

Hummers sometimes entered the greenhouses Blincoes operated for years and fed on the flowers. Often, if it were difficult to reach the tiny insects on which they fed, they tore the blossoms to shreds with their long beaks.

This lack of control affects their family life. After an elaborate courtship that involves spectacular flights in which both sexes participate, the male goes off, footloose and fancy free, leaving the female to build the nest and rear their young alone.

The nest is a jewel, too, a tiny one-inch in diameter cup made of plant down held

S   U   M

together by flower scales and lichens and secured to a small branch or twig by spider webs. It is dainty, exquisite but deceptively strong, for it is often used by a second and, rarely, a third brood.

Of course the babies, usually two, never more, are exceedingly small, no larger than a pea and are fed partially digested food by regurgitation, a truly formidable proceeding. Imagine pumping food into such minute creatures with a long, sharp beak.

From deep throated flowers, columbine, nasturtiums, trumpet vine, etc., hummers feed on tiny insects and nectar. It is believed now that hummers might have attained their preference for nectar from probing for insect fare. These fascinating little creatures may be attracted to our gardens by man-made feeders containing a sweetened liquid food.

We now know that hummingbirds are here in spring long before they visit the flowers blooming in our gardens. They return early and feed on the greenish bloom of deciduous trees in our forests, at such a height that their presence is not suspected.

The largest flock of hummingbirds I ever saw was about 25, all young of the year, feeding on jewel weed. This flower has a strong attraction for this small bird.

M   E   R

August's gold

Gold! Pure gold! The sparkling coins spill over acres of space, glowing, each round disk receiving and casting back its rich glitter from its source, the great sun.

For gold is the predominating color on the prairie at Aullwood. The flowers tower to great height to compete with the tall grasses. Blue stem grass stands nine feet high and is still growing. Compass plant, one of the three tallest flowering plants, looks it straight in the face, its stem thick as one's arm and straight as an arrow. Its leaves are intricately cut. These leaves take a north-south position on the stem, hence the name, compass plant. The surface of the entire plant is rough, bristly.

Prairie dock is distinguished by its enormous basal leaves. They are slightly heart shaped, dock-like, often two feet long and correspondingly wide. One is surprised that plants the size of compass plant and prairie dock produce flowers that are small with ragged rays. The effect is similar to that of hearing a powerfully built man speak with a high falsetto voice.

Perhaps the most beautiful of these tall flowers is the coreopsis. Its deeply cut leaves give the plant a daintiness lacking in the rather coarse prairie flowers and it is topped by a panicle of flowers, each about two inches across. The center disk is brown and the golden rays are broad and regular, giving the flower a finished perfection.

Most prairie flowers are composites, flowers having a central disk with petals or rays like the daisy's. There are many other showy golden flowers, coneflowers, rosin weed, sunflowers and goldenrods, which are not yet blooming. They do not grow so tall, but nevertheless, make an imposing display.

Rosin weed grows in a unique way. The stem is long and the flowers bloom loosely at the top. But the leaves give it a special interest: they grow in pairs, two facing east-west, the next pair, slightly below, north-south and follow this procedure down the entire stem. The effect is attractive, as well as practical, for in this exposure, the leaves receive adequate light, air and moisture, growing as they do surrounded by dense grasses.

To break the preponderance of golden color, there are stately stalks of purple *liatris*, the large purple coneflower, a smattering of the pure whiteness of flowering spurge, the oddity of rattlesnake master, a flower that grows like the yucca with an umbel of off-white flower heads. The tall bush clover is a quaint clover we all should learn to know. It has clublike greenish white heads made up of tiny florets, each having a purple throat.

The flowers of the prairie hold one spellbound, but the real pull of the prairie lies in its grasses. The big blue stem is gorgeous but not overwhelming. An isolated clump shows up its subtle grayish blue stem, its graceful masculine strength. Switchgrass with its large, lacy plume, showing both male and female flowers, and Canada nodding rye with its full-blown flower heads, all add variety to prairie plant life.

To see the prairie as the sun rises, illuminating each heavy drop of dew clinging to millions of blades of grass with iridescent light that gleams and dances with every movement of hot August air, fills one's mind and spirit with reverence and praise. The tiny dewdrops on the garden spider's gossamer web, so delicate yet so enduring, show up an architecture man can never emulate. There comes the sweet, tremulous morning song of the field sparrow, a song of gratitude for a new day, a song of hope.

S U M

Seed survival

It is the ambition of all plants to produce seeds that will insure their survival in a competitive natural environment. There are many examples of how this obsessive force demonstrates itself within the plant.

Chicory grew in my lawn many years ago when it was farm land. Some chicory still comes up in the grass even though I constantly try to get rid of it. Left undisturbed, chicory grows to a height of three or four feet.

Mowing cuts it down so that it never grows taller than the grass, yet down at ground level I often find the pretty lavender-blue flower in full bloom, striving in its own driving determination, against all handicaps, to produce seeds for its own perpetuation. Other wild plants, Queen Anne's lace, wild asters, hairy rhuella and many other plants in mowed-over areas, follow the same behavior pattern.

Mature seeds of wild plants have uncanny ways of distribution. They evidently are important in nature's broad plan, for ways of getting from one place to another are part of their innate equipment for travel. There are those plants whose seeds are attached to dainty parachutes of silken fluff that are carried great distances by all the winds that blow.

They are, to name a few, dandelion, goat's beard, wild lettuce, thistle, milkweed and one notorious nuisance, the sand vine, which produces a beautiful seed pod and seeds similar to those of the milkweed. On these wind-borne parachutes the ripe seed points downward and when it lands its sharp tip penetrates the soil, thus placing it in an advantageous position for germination.

I have mentioned before the handsome nodding thistle that suddenly appeared in my lawn. I wish it were possible to trace it to its place of origin in order to estimate how many miles the seed was carried. The closest record I have of the nodding thistle is a country road in Clark County en route to Cedar Bog.

Then there are seeds that cling. You start out on a field trip neat as the proverbial pin. You return looking bedraggled, your clothing covered with the flat three-cornered seeds of the tick trefoil. A common and appropriate name is stick tight, for it really does. The parent plant, tick trefoil, is attractive and bears a beautiful little flower shaped like the cultivated sweet pea. How it ever produces such a strange, devious seed is a mystery. The stick tight is seldom seen, yet you can't avoid it and you're only aware of it at your walk's end when you start planting it for next year's growth by scraping it off your clothing and by letting the seeds fall where they will.

Burs are distributed in the same way tick trefoil travels. Cockle burs (two species) and burdock burs are covered with hooked bristles that cling to human clothing and the hair of mammals. They are planted when the carrier rids itself of them. Cockle burs are often swept along by flooded streams and grow rankly on flood plains.

Many plants produce conventional seeds that stay put on the parent plant and are eaten directly from the plant by birds. Undigested seeds from fruit and berries are scattered abroad by birds and grow from the birds' droppings.

We know that the blue jay actually plants beech nuts and acorns in the woods. Squirrels do not eat all the nuts they lay away for winter food and they eventually grow. All these interrelated incidents in food planting and distribution join to make the interdependence between the plant and animal one of the most interesting stories in nature.

Autumn

The morns are meeker than they were
The nuts are turning brown
The berry's cheek is plumper
The rose is out of town.

The maple wears a gayer scarf,
The field, a scarlet gown.
Lest I should be old-fashioned,
I'll put a trinket on.

Emily Dickinson

Fall's insects

"The katydid says it as plain as can be
And the cricket is chirping it under the tree.
In the aster's blue eye you can read the
same hint
Just as clearly as if you had seen it in print,
And the corn sighs it, too, as it waves in the
Sun
That autumn is here and summer is done."

Insects have their heyday in autumn. They are articulate both day and night. They are not easily seen at anytime, however, and when I say this I immediately think of exceptions: mosquitoes, ants, flies, bees. But grasshoppers will illustrate the point I am trying to make.

Out in the field, a grasshopper may fly past you, entirely visible. But try to find it after it has made its landing. It's like trying to find the proverbial needle in a haystack. Most insects have the protective earth colors of their environment and do a convincing disappearing act as they blend into the greens, browns and tans of the meadows.

The praying mantis is one of our most dramatic insects. It is unique in its physical appearance, with spiny, foreshortened front legs, an abnormally long tubular thorax and an elongated slender abdomen. Its wings are long, gauzy. It looks a lot like Kermit, the Muppet, in the face, without any of Kermit's appeal. It is the only insect that can look at you "over its shoulder," for it is able to turn its head. It is fierce, cannibalistic in its feeding habits. Once captured, its victim seldom escapes.

Recently I saw a half-grown mantis bite off more than he could chew. We were walking a trail in the prairie at Aullwood when nearby we heard the ear-splitting cry of a cicada. Paul Knoop's sharp eyes quickly found the cicada in the grasp of the mantis. The victim — big, strong, its body covered by plates, like armor — was putting up a desperate struggle to free itself, rattling its castanets of sound and maneuvering its body in desperation. The mantis, worn out with the struggle, must have weakened its grip for an instant and the cicada, taking instinctive advantage of the reprieve, managed to break loose and zoom off.

Insects are vocal creatures. Their songs, drones, chirps and buzzes are lost to most human ears during the day as they must compete with the cacophony of sounds made by man.

Conditions change at night, however, when noise of the workaday world subsides, freed for awhile from the barrage of man-made clangor. Then the insect orchestration takes over. The trained entomologist can identify individual songs.

But a few common insect songs can be isolated from the general chorus and soon are easily recognized.

The katydid leads the night insect chorus as surely as the robin carries the burden of early morning bird song. In both cases they provide the background music. The katydid's voice is a decisive, emphatic, "ka-ty-did" with the accent on the last syllable. We are all probably familiar with the old prophecy that we'll have frost six weeks after we hear the first katydid sing.

The katydid is a nile green grasshopper with antennae longer than the body, very handsome and well protected in its leafy habitat by its coloration.

When day breaks, the lively, rhythmical insect music ceases. Then our attention centers on insects that we are attracted to by sight rather than sound — butterflies floating like bright colored gauze as they search for goldenrod, butterfly weed and butterfly bush in cultivated gardens; dragonflies as they dart over bogs, wet fields and along farm ponds.

A   U   T

Blue jay

He's screaming from the woodlots now, screeching in the orchards, accusing anyone within range of his voice of being a thief and, from the dense shrubbery in our backyard, comes his gentle *sotto voce* "tea kettle" or "teekle" song. That handsome rogue, the blue jay!

A score of adjectives might be used to describe him with a noun or two thrown in for good measure, very few complimentary. He's used to name calling, however, for he's a controversial bird. Some folks have little use for him, while others find him one of our most interesting American birds and certainly one of the most handsome.

Noisy, brassy, lawless, impudent, sassy, swashbuckling, thieving, bold, mischievous, you could go on and on and not entirely encompass his wide latitude of traits, abilities and offenses. He is branded as a thief and murderer, an outlaw without regard for the rights of others in the avian community.

In many cases he's been tried and convicted without proper evidence or trial by jury.

He's never been called a sneak, however, for he scorns the devious. Intrigue and the oblique approach are lacking in his character. The only time in the entire year when he's quiet and skulks is that period when he's molting. What a humiliating time that is for this handsome, proud Beau Brummell! Scruffy body feathers, feathers missing from wings and tail, to say nothing of skin actually showing around the neck, make him look like a disheveled, scrawny tramp.

Now that he's well groomed again, he's vocal and wandering all over the country showing off his good looks.

Ever since the settling of our land the blue jay has been accused of stealing other birds' eggs and eating young birds in the nest. Years ago Prof. Beal, of the Fish and Wildlife Service, Department of Agriculture, and an eminent scientific analyst, found on examining the stomach contents of 292 blue jays that "remains of birds were found in only 2 and the shells of bird's eggs in 3." He concluded "the accusation of eating eggs and young birds is certainly not sustained and it is futile to attempt to reconcile the conflicting statements on this point until more accurate observations have been made."

Observers have never seen any dramatic courtship display performed by these birds but much information about the affection and devotion of mated pairs and their devotion to their young has been gathered.

Years ago a pair nested in an old apple tree close to our kitchen window. We watched the male help construct the sturdy, well built nest. He was always nearby, usually in the next tree, on guard. He often fed his brooding mate. Frequently he shoved her off the nest as if urging her to go for exercise and food while he watched and kept the eggs warm.

"He has virtues, I can list them
(Though his enemies will twist them)
And his scintillating blueness
Brings the sky, on wings, to me.
In some way the rascal tethers
Me with chains of bright blue feathers."

B. Y. Williams

U   M   N

Killdeer

Charadrius vociferous! That's my killdeer! And he was living up to his name this bright invigorating morning. An adult pair wheeled and soared overhead, tall treetop high, calling excitedly as they flew.

A quality of urgency and concern was evident in their voices as they circled over a long narrow field where a neighbor's palomino grazed.

Occasionally they dropped lower, with wings pointed downward as if about to alight. In this position they uttered a long trilling "t-r-rrrrr." Then with a sudden burst of speed they shot upward, shouting "kill-dee, kill-dee, kill-dee" so loudly they could have been heard a mile away.

Off they flew to the north and as I watched they turned back and flew, banking and skimming low over the field, calling more softly now, in coaxing tones, "kill-dee-ah, kill-dee-ah."

An answering call came from the ground and, as if given courage as well as encouragement from their parents, three young killdeers rose into the air and followed the old birds the length of the field, turned and returned to the spot from which they had taken off.

Here the vegetation was sparse and I could plainly see all five birds carrying on with the wildest enthusiasm, the young ones running a few steps, stopping to look about, heads bobbing, tails twitching in the teetering, nervous manner of plovers, and then running off again, chattering and "deeing" as if they accomplished the impossible.

The old birds were equally articulate, calling and rattling off congratulations for a job well done. I had witnessed the first flight of a brood of young killdeers!

From the moment the killdeer arrives in the spring, and he is an early bird, returning to our valley as early as the first week in February, until he leaves us sometime in the fall, we know he is around.

There is nothing retiring about this plover. He arrives shouting. He drops down into sparse grassland or plowed fields that have lain fallow through the winter and runs about screaming "kill-deer, kill-deer" at the top of his voice. He can be heard flying over during the night, his loud voice threatening to kill his dear.

Even during nesting, the killdeer will run screaming from his nest feigning injury, by dragging a wing or leg, all the time leading you away from his nest with heart-rending "dees."

Killdeers gather in flocks along shores of lakes and farm ponds, nervous, jittery, and keep up a querulous "dee-dee-dee."

You can approach them stealthily and see them all spread out on the feeding grounds.

One spots you.

He lets out a wild, ear-splitting "dee-dee-dee" and then they all rise as if on a single pair of wings, wheeling and turning about in the sky.

They make a great to-do but they really are not afraid at all. Seeing us is something to get excited about and they seem to thrive on excitement. Soon they all return to the very spot from which they flew.

Most killdeer fly to the southern part of the country for the winter. But for several years we've found killdeers on the Christmas bird count. It's almost unbelievable that this insectivorous bird can find sustenance suffucent for survival along the frozen waterways and snow-covered fields. It's the only time throughout the year, however, that he doesn't find much to shout about.

A   U   T

Man-made prairie

The prairie has always been a place of wonder and excitement. Exposed to the unobstructed power of the sun, forever tossed about by every wind that blew across the land, it extended from Indiana to the Rockies, from Manitoba to Texas, a waving, flowing sea of grass.

Antelope loped gracefully across its plain, finding easy food. Untold thousands of buffalo thundered across its unlimited expanse and the Indians followed, for the buffalo provided them their basic needs: food, clothing and shelter. Down in the rich grasses the prairie dog tunneled his villages.

France owned this vast land interlaced with lazy rivers. Napoleon Bonaparte needed money for his war-mongering and in 1803 sold it to the United States for $15,000,000 — quite a real estate deal.

Then the rape of the prairie began.

Lewis and Clark explored it and reported its riches to our government. Mountain men started the ultimate extermination of the beaver and other fur-bearing animals. Early settlers, looking for new horizons, started West, traveling in covered wagons through grasses that grew taller than the wagons. Then gold was discovered and the rush was on. The railroads followed. Carl Sandburg, son of the prairie, wrote:

A thousand redmen cried and went away to new places for corn and their women.
A million white men came and put up skyscrapers
Threw out rails and wires, feelers to the salt sea.
Now the smokestacks bite the skyline with stub teeth.

Most of the true prairie has been turned under by the plow to form the vast farms where corn and wheat grow in such quantity that the area is known as the breadbasket of the world. At the same time the farm practices set the scene for the dreadful dust storms of the 1930s.

The vast buffalo herds are gone, killed inhumanely for their hides. When the first railroads opened sportsmen rode the trains and shot buffalo feeding on the prairie, leaving their bodies to rot in the sun as the trains passed.

But man can make a prairie, a sea of grass, and it has been successfully accomplished in our own community. It is a small prairie where one buffalo would create havoc, a colony of prairie dogs would do serious damage and where a wigwam dwelling Indian would start chanting "don't fence me in!"

This small gem of a prairie flourishes at Aullwood Audubon Center and right now is at the peak of its interest and beauty.

The prairie was started in 1959 and by 1974 was extended to 10 acres with the plantings finished. Seeds of true prairie plants were obtained from Lynx prairie in Adams County, Ohio, and from a true prairie in Illinois.

A tower at Aullwood allows the visitor to see the entire prairie at a glance: The tall grasses waving in rhythm to the wind's blowing, the flowering plants flaunting their bright fall color.

There is the bluestem grass towering straight and tall, the graceful, drooping plumes of uniola grass, buffalo grass and Indian grass.

Some prairie plants are amazing in height, like the prairie dock with its enormous leaves and the compass plant with its large, deeply cut leaves. The seed heads of these plants are even more interesting than the flowers. The stiff goldenrod is a rare prairie plant with lovely individual florets on a flat umbel.

Zoo trip

I've been to Cincinnati many times, always with an escort or a group of friends. All I had to do was go, with an assurance of a good time in pleasant company. We drove down in cars, each driver knowing his way about, all details wrapped up in a neat package without a single responsibility on my part.

Today, however, was different. Joey, my 10-year-old grandson, and I were going to Cincinnati on the bus because Gram never learned to drive a car. Of course we were going to the zoo and to Eden Park to visit the conservatory. I never knew a 10-year-old boy who didn't like animals, but Joey likes plants, too, so the conservatory was a must.

Now Gram is the least sophisticated traveler in America, has no sense of direction and can get lost in a supermarket, so she had doubts about finding her way in a big city. But we managed. We learned right off that we had to have a lot of quarters, dimes and nickels to ride the Metro. We learned right off that people are kind and want to help two strangers at the opposite ends of the age bracket who came to their city for a fun day. We had a grand time, partly because Joey always knew where he was — and just as importantly — where he had been.

We made a bee-line for the zoo and were at the gate when it opened. On our way there, we talked about the animal we'd like best to see and decided on the giraffe. We started at Entrance I and what did we see first? The giraffes, of course, father, mother, baby (so young and new his umbilical cord was still attached) and an older brother. Who could ask for a better start to a day of new sights and wonders?

We took a ride on the little train that gives a preview of the grounds, visited the outdoor exhibits, drooled over the white tiger and the cheetahs, felt sorry for the lion crouched in a corner of the man-made run he called home, and fell in love with the animals of the veldt, so far away from their native land.

Two inside exhibits, the aquarium and the new insect building, were the highlights of our zoo visit. The insect exhibit is superb.

The entrance to the Insect Building is unimpressive, for you have the feeling you're walking into the hill, as if following the Pied Piper of Hamelin. Once inside, however, you are struck by the creative imagination and artistry that govern its design as well as the practicality of the display areas. For example, the idea of placing the rooms underground assures a mean temperature the year round which aids laboratory work and safeguards the preservation of the mounted specimens, which are in perfect condition and mounted with great technical skill.

One feature I especially like here is the magnifying glasses that slide along on a track above the mounted specimens, enlarging each fragile butterfly and moth scale, compound eyes, spines on the hind legs of grasshoppers and crickets, the veins in transparent wings.

This exhibit, being new, attracted a large crowd and it was difficult to study it as closely as I would have liked. I thought that the flow of traffic should have been regulated better as people advanced from

A   U   T

opposite directions and caused congestion and irritation, particularly among those seriously interested in entomology.

I also was disappointed that there were no live exhibits showing the life cycle (metamorphosis) of species. It would be easy to find all phases of the life processes of the Cecropia moth, one of our common handsome night flying moths, whose larva, a good looker in its own right, spins a silken cocoon. Also many colorful butterflies are easily obtained, particularly the Monarch butterfly whose larva and chrysalis are especially beautiful.

Eden Park is well-named. Its hills are crowned with fine forest trees and its man-made lake is a cup reflecting the blue sky. The Conservatory with its tumbling waterfall that forms a wee brook that winds through the high domed section of the building is pure delight. Here are tropical plants with many varieties of palm, showing the versatility of this species. One section displays plants having brilliant foliage, another cacti and succulents.

We climbed the highest hilltop in the park and sat on a bench in the cooling shade of the great trees. They were so tall the shade filtered through, light, airy as lace. We were tired, surfeited with all we'd seen and done. Jays called. Cicadas made our ears ring with their singing.

"What sound do you hear, Joey?" I asked.

"Tractor mowing grass," answered Joey with a mischievous twinkle in his eye.

"Now Joey," Gram protested.

"Locusts," said Joey.

"Cicadas," corrected Gram.

U   M   N

Town birds

So often we hear people say they would like to know more about birds but they live in town, do not get out to the country often, and therefore have no opportunity to see and study them.

This is true only to a certain degree, for there are many birds to see in the city, sometimes the business district (and I am not referring to pigeons and starlings), and residential areas have many appealing species in their yards and gardens.

There is one bird we purposely come to town to see. I refer to the nighthawk. It nests on the flat graveled roofs of business buildings. We are greatly attracted to this handsome, superb flyer and like to drive to a spot where we can watch several zig-zag through the evening sky showing their long powerful wings with the bold, broad white "underline" through the center.

We enjoy the nighthawk's loud, harsh call, "peent, peent" as it courses after the insects on which it feeds. It must consume prodigious amounts of food in order to supply the energy needed for its long air-borne hours.

Chimney swifts, too, like the town and we see more over the rooftops of city streets than we do in rural areas. Walk along our rivers in town any day and you will be rewarded by seeing swifts and several species of swallows skim low over the water feeding on emerging insects and barely touching the surface of the water for a drink and a quick bath.

While you watch, pleased with the skill, grace and speed of these small birds, you might hear the rattle of the queer, top-heavy kingfisher as he barges downstream.

Our rivers have attracted many species of ducks, the cunning coot, the alert little grebes, both the herring and ringbilled gulls, and terns. During the summer the little green heron hunts through the sunny day in the shallows along shore and our rivers have played host to night herons and those exotic wanderers from the southland, the American egret.

Perhaps the most outstanding downtown visitors ever to venture within the confines of the city are the exciting avocets, the large shorebirds with the turned-up beaks, from out West.

One day as we drove down Catalpa Drive we had a city bird observation that delighted us, it was so unique and humorous. We stopped for traffic and in the yard on the corner a wrought iron name plate proclaimed ownership. As we waited, a beautiful sparrow hawk flew into the yard and perched on the name plate not more than three feet from the ground.

He was right at home, tail twitching, head bent as if searching for a dancing grasshopper. There was traffic noise from the street, lawnmowers cluttering the air with sound, there were shouts and cries of children playing all around, yet the bird was undisturbed, unafraid.

Here was a bird of prey, a species that customarily hovers over vast country fields looking for rodent victims, that had evidently adapted himself to life in a closely built-up city community.

One time on the corner of Third and Main I chanced to look up in time to see a great blue heron sail majestically across town. I have heard the song sparrow sing in the grounds around the Old Courthouse. Perhaps there are more interesting bird observations awaiting those who stop and look and listen "where they are."

A　　　　　U　　　　　T

Fringed gentian

Many years ago after I'd passed the time when, as a student, I regarded the late Professor Werthner in awe and progressed to a relaxed friendship in which we shared a mutual love of the outdoors, I discovered he had a secret. He knew where fringed gentians grew and he was not about to share that knowledge with anyone.

Even that long ago the flowers were rare. The wet woods, the bogs, marsh lands and swamps where they grew were being drained to make more land suitable for farming and to meet the needs of Dayton as an expanding manufacturing city.

Even then, poorly informed people were guilty of picking them and transplanting them to home gardens where they promptly died. For where is there a gardener capable of creating such a specific environment as these loveliest of all wild flowers need? Realizing their danger Prof. Werthner never revealed the place where these flowers could be found in the Dayton vicinity.

So the years went by and I never saw fringed gentians until I had my first autumn visit to Cedar Bog. There, one October day when the air was so clear the sun cast shadows black as night along the road and in the fence rows, we stepped out into an open wet field and, to our wonder and delight, there was spread before us the rare beauty of the fringed gentians I had for such a long time longed to see.

The plants stood about 18 inches tall, full of bloom, the flowers such an indescribable shade of blue that they moved one with deep emotion and stirred the imagination as no more abundant flower ever could. Here before me lay the end of my search, the fulfillment of a wish that had eluded me for years. The matchless blue, the delicacy of each fringed petal, the serene perfection of the flower far surpassed the long anticipation.

Much has been written about the wondrous blue of the fringed gentian. Bryant wrote about its coming when "the aged year is at its end."

Then doth thy sweet and quiet eye
Look through its fringes at the sky.
Blue — blue — as if that sky let fall
A flower from its cerulean wall.

But the fringed gentian is not sky-blue. A bit of deep-violet in the blue gives it a misty delicate quality of coloring not measured by the poet or artist.

The preservation of this rare wildling is a tenuous thing. It is an annual and depends on the effectual dispersal of seeds to insure succession of growth. Picking the flowers prevents seed formation, so they should never be disturbed.

Fringed gentians have been successfully established in the small swamp at the Audubon Center. Year after year in October's bright blue weather they lift their blue faces to the blue autumn sky.

It is no secret, inaccessible place where their existence is threatened, but a happy, generous place where one can drink deep of their unique beauty and rejoice that they are safe.

U   M   N

Monarch butterfly

It flew from the field across the road, fresh as new birth, strong, with a strength given to some creatures of delicate structure, beautiful as October, for it is October's child, this Monarch butterfly, burnt orange with black lines and spots pure white.

Now it was past me, flying fairly high, heading directly south, steady as to direction but battling a frisky breeze that tossed its weightless body off a straight-line course.

We see southbound Monarch butterflies every year at this time. I report their passing in this column. Its life history is unique, it plays out its role in nature with a regularity that never fails and its appearance, its summer presence, and its autumnal migration are as dependable as is the smooth operation of the universe of which it is such a fragile part.

How can I give it its deserved "place in the sun," how can I portray the unique quality of this single insect out of nearly a million species of insects that exist in our world, without boring repetition?

The amazing, the awesome thing about this brilliant butterfly is the clocklike mechanism that governs its entire life forces — its mating, its egg bearing, its existence as larva or caterpillar, the miracle of forming its chrysalis before our wondering eyes. This chrysalis is a structure that certainly must be one of the most perfectly beautiful things found in nature, elegant in shape and proportion, lovely in color — Nile green with a row of the tiniest golden dots around the enlarged, rounded upper portion. A noted entomologist described it as "a tiny green casket with golden nails." The emergence of the mature butterfly in about two weeks is another miracle, for if it emerges in early autumn it is of a special brood.

Monarch butterflies probably produce several broods during the summer, for eggs are laid on the underside of milkweed leaves as early as the plant matures. This butterfly brings pleasure during the summer but the Monarchs that are bred in September are destined to perpetuate the race as they begin their migration south almost immediately. This is why they are so perfect as we see them now, their wings unfrayed by wind and weather, and evidently tough and strong.

Their flight is unhurried, they stop to rest, often massed in impressive numbers in some small tree or shrub, then continue on to the warm southland where they congregate in vast numbers on special trees they find to their liking. There are established wintering places in California, Florida and Mexico just over the Texas border. Perhaps there are other undiscovered wintering places in southern areas.

In spring these wintering Monarchs start north, the time coinciding with the time the milkweed plants start growing. The females deposit their eggs on the host plant, thus starting a new generation and, having fulfilled their destiny, they die.

All butterflies and their allies, the moths, have their own peculiar host plant. The interrelation is fixed and both the plant and insect profit by the association: the insect finds safety and food for its young; the flowers of the plant are fertilized by the feeding habits of the insect. Some have more than one plant on which they can depend for food. For example, the Cecropia moth feeds on apple, maple and lilac leaves.

A   U   T

But the Monarch feeds exclusively on the milkweed. Most butterfly larvae and cocoons are earth-colored gray, brown, grayish brown for protection.

Consider how the Monarch in every phase of its development "walks in beauty." It is one of our handsomest butterflies, bold in color that is striking in late summer wandering. The female instinctively selects a distinguished plant for a host. The milkweed is tall, strong with thick milky leaves and flower clusters of small, complex flowerets that produce the attractive rough, gray-green seed pods. The eggs are waxen, ivory colored, truly beautiful and the caterpillars are stunning, with alternate bands of black and off-white with a

greenish yellow cast. They raise the fore segments of their bodies to ward off enemies and threateningly move their antennae in a way that frightens birds. The Monarch is offensive to the taste and leads a charmed life with this built-in defense against many enemies.

Year after year with the precision and regularity of nature's functioning in a universe operating under immutable laws, we see the recurring wonder and beauty of this unique insect. We are awed when we consider that the Creator of a universe so vast, so complex we cannot comprehend it, has also created a creature of such frail strength and simple appeal that it is equally incomprehensible.

U   M   N

Wasps

Wasps are architects of competence and imagination. They are engineers of ingenuity and precision. They are builders of skill and dedication.

Two building materials are used, wood and mud. The wood, they miraculously change to paper and, from the mud, they make fine clay structures of beauty and endurance.

Mud daubers are wasps that build nests of mud, but "dauber" belies the connotation we usually give the word, for all the nests I've examined made of mud are meticulously sculptured without any sign of the careless workmanship of a "dauber."

But it is the large hanging nest of the paper wasp that captures the wonder and admiration of the naturalist. These are made by two species of hornets, the bald-faced hornet and the yellow jacket. There are two species of yellow jackets, one being the small wasp that invites himself to our picnic table, sips fruit juices and sits on the edge of the plate and daintily feeds on anything he can reach before you wave him away with an indignant but timorous hand. This enterprising fellow builds an underground nest which the casual observer seldom sees.

A larger yellow jacket and the bald-faced hornet build bulky nests firmly around and anchored to branches of large deciduous trees. The branches form a framework for the nest and hold it together so effectively it is not disturbed or damaged when buffeted by the severest summer storms. Sometimes, but not commonly, these large nests are built on walls protected by wide overhanging eaves.

When completed, the paper wasp's nest is a thing of beauty. The texture of the paper is rough, colored with swirls of blended tan, white and light brown. Some are of contrasting tones of gray and white. We had a large and especially handsome nest in the Dayton Museum of Natural History collection that was the softest gray with occasional swirls of rose color.

Paper wasps have sharp, strong toothed jaws. We can scarcely comprehend the power of these working tools. The wasp flies to some well seasoned wood, an unpainted fence or outbuilding, bites off a tiny piece and chews it. A chemical in the saliva changes the wood to paper. The liquid mass, now building material, is used to construct the fabulous nest.

Many wasps work together at the construction. They are a highly organized, well disciplined colony made up of workers, and drones, governed by a queen. Nests vary in size determined by the number of workers serving the queen.

The nest consists of several tiers of cells, hexagonal in size, like those formed in honey combs in beehives, the difference being that the honey comb is made of wax, the wasp cells made of paper. The cells are made of paper of a tougher, thicker

honey or syrup made from brown sugar. The food those larvae fed on must have been a delectable ambrosia!

On the queen's nuptial flight her eggs are fertilized and they are fertile to the end of her life even though she may live several years and mother many colonies of wasps. In each cell she deposits an egg, and even though the nest hangs down, a gluey substance on the surface of the egg holds it in place.

In two or three days a small larva is hatched from the egg and a tiny sticky disc on its rear end fastens the little fellow face front to its snug cell. Now a busy time starts for the workers. All these babies must be fed and it's their job to feed them. They find small soft insects and spiders, chew them and feed the partially digested food to the small grubs whose hungry mouths are open at each cell.

Somewhere, among the hundreds of cells, particular cells, a third larger than those of the workers, house larvae that will receive special food and care. They will become new young queens.

When the larvae are full grown they make a cocoon and enter the pupa stage of their development. The workers seal each cell with a snug fitting lid. When the metamorphosis is complete the young wasps chew their way through the lid and leave the nest either to enlarge the parent nest or to form a new colony.

consistency than that of the outside covering of the nest. The nest hangs downward with an opening near the bottom and a little to one side where wasps enter and leave.

We once cut open the nest of a bald-faced hornet at the museum which showed the amazing structure of the tiers and cells. We were surprised at the delightful odor that emanated from the interior. It smelled like

Glory of trees

"The glory of trees is more than their gifts." At no other time of the year is this more apparent than it is in October.

We forget then the tree's ultimate service — providing wood for shelter from heat or cold or a fire in the hearth, food to sustain the body, paper for feeding mind and spirit, furniture for living and shade from summer's sun.

It is the glory that counts, and in October we behold the glory. It is in the flame of the maple and sour gum, the yellow of hickory and basswood, the bronze of oak and beech, the rosy red of dogwood and sumac, the fine purplish glow of some ashes and the indescribable combination of yellow, red and orange that some maples paint with such breathtaking effect. Sassafras and sweet gum, too, mix these colors on the artist's easel and add their particular glory to October's kaleidoscope of color.

All too soon the brilliance falls to carpet the forest floor, to wash sidewalks of city streets with color or make a puddle of massed beauty on the home lawn. What a way to go, to face death with magnificent proof that there is no death, that the leaves recreate life anew by their dissolution and return again in trees and flowers and flowing sweep of grass.

The forests of the northern hemisphere would not be able to stage such a colossal color show were it not for the maples. They are the fortissimo of the artist's brush. They are distributed all over the northern world, nearly a hundred species with only one species being found south of the equator, in Java.

Ohio has only six native maples: red, black, scarlet, silver, sugar and the maverick, the ash-leaved maple known as the box elder. Only the black maple, which looks so much like the sugar maple, is scarce. Many other maples have been introduced, and they have added to the diversity and beautification of our city streets and home grounds.

Maples are easily transplanted. Our native maples, with the possible exception of the box elder, grow to tremendous size. Almost every community can point with pride to individual trees of great girth and height.

Acer is the family name of the maple. The silver maple is *acer saccharinum,* so named because the sap is sweet. The sugar maple is *acer saccharum,* also meaning sweet, which can be confusing even to those who insist on using scientific names. The confusion is enhanced when we learn that all maple is sweet.

But only the sap of the sugar maple flows so freely and with such volume that it makes commercial production of maple sugar and syrup possible. Maple syrup was the only source of sugar the early New England colonists had. They learned how to produce it from the Indians.

Perhaps the sugar maple is the most important member of its family. Its aesthetic worth cannot be estimated, but its wood is excellent for building and making furniture. All maples, excepting the silver maple, are hard. They grow slowly and are hardy and long lasting. Silver maple grows fast and reaches great height, but the wood is brittle and breaks easily in storm winds.

A　　　　　U　　　　　T

Power of hills

A wise man once wrote, "As mankind's capacity for awe contracts, mankind is diminished." There are manifestations in nature that overcome sensitive man with awe. These manifestations need not have been created on a vast scale. The grandeur of Mount Hood is no more awe-inspiring than the exquisite texture and beauteous coloring found in the scale of a butterfly's wing viewed under a microscope. The human reaction to both experiences is relative, but the awe remains and consequently the observer in beholding has grown in empathy and understanding, not diminished.

The diminishing comes when he walks in beauty and doesn't see it, or, which is sadder still, on seeing is indifferent or unstirred.

Last weekend I stood on the top of a high hill. Below on its slope extended a prairie meadow where little bluestem grass, full-ripened now and showing faint tufts of white in its mature seed heads, waved in a gentle breeze. In spring and early summer this grass is a rich blue-green which gives it its common name. It is true prairie grass. Now it is dull bronze and blends agreeably with the autumnal tints of New England aster's purple-blue, the lavender and white of other species of aster, the fading gold of goldenrod, the bright disks of black-eyed Susan and the smaller thin-leafed coneflower.

It is a treasured spot. I've seen it awaken to life in spring. One summer I made a survey of its rich plant life, its nesting bird population and listed the birds singing in its surrounding forest. I have never seen it in its time of winter rest. On this fall day I soaked up the warmth of the October sun, viewed the panorama of autumn color, the vast sweep of its white cloud-clotted blue sky, from its crest.

Down in the narrow valley the farmland lay warm and content. The snug, attractive farm house on one farm has a new roof and as the spouting catches the sunlight, it glances off and deflects rays in all directions. Proud little house!

About 50 sheep graze on one green slope and high above the house a field of corn has been harvested and the lines of cornstalk "wigwams" stand straight and severe against the background of forest. A big red barn and several smaller outbuildings painted white cluster near the house, but in the high field a tall old building weathered gray stands alone.

My gaze lifts to the horizon to the fold of hills, tree crowned, still green with only a hint of yellow in tulip poplar and hickory. The hills! Their unchanging strength, their unshakable calm, their vast folds, a line of darker green that marks a rift in a ridge and indicates a gorge or narrow valley, carved by some swift creek that cuts its way to join Brush Creek that in turn hurries to join the broad Ohio.

What power the hills have to restore the bruised, troubled spirit of man! Yet how small a mere human appears against their majesty, their mystic silence and serenity. Unless he is completely callous he stands in awe.

Then I remembered a poem, *Great Wide World*, I learned in the third grade. It extolled the beauties and wonders of the world, but in order not to overwhelm the small child with his own insignificance compared to the greatness of the world, the poet ended his poem comfortingly:

You are more than the earth though you're such a dot,
You can love and think and the earth can not.

Night sounds

We lose much of interest in the world about us by sleeping through the night. This was proven to us the night we spent in the Adams County hills recently. There is the music of insects that sing in the night. How few of us can identify insects by sound. Who can tell the difference between the music of the toad and frog, ah, who has trained his ear, his mind, his emotion to the place he even recognizes it as music?

Who can distinguish the difference between the bark of a fox hunting in the night and the yap of a wakeful farm dog?

There are the smells of the night wafted to you on the winds of darkness that titillate the senses in a way sun-warmed fragrances never do. There is the mysterious sough of the wind in the treetops, the sigh of light breezes we hear only because of the quiet of the night, stilled by the absence of the cacophony of sound created by the daytime busyness of man.

There is the beauty of the night sky. The full moon, the stars riding the dark dome of heaven, their light casting black shadows on the earth and falling bright on narrow valleys while the hills loom huge and protective in the magic light.

You are bemused by the mystery of night, its lights, its shadows, its scents and sounds.

Sleep eludes you. So you join a small group, armed with powerful flashlights and a tape recorder of owl calls, that is attempting to entice owls to nearby trees. The recorder is turned on and the quavering call of the screech owl is released on the quiet of the woods.

The recorder is turned off and we hear an answering owl call. A dark form, wings wide and silent, for a moment is silhouetted against the dim light of the sky, then flies to a tree overhead. A play of the flashlight reveals a screech owl peering down toward the light.

Three screech owls responded to our recording and another member of our party heard the barred owl, the real "hoot" owl of its clan, farther off in the forest.

Owls are hunters of the night. The eyes with their enormous pupils enable owls to see well in the dark. Their hearing is extremely keen, their flight is unerring and silent.

Equipped with needle sharp talons and strong tearing beaks they hunt animal food in the woods. They prey on the old, the infirm, the unwary, those animals unable to make a clean getaway. Thus the fittest survive, an inexorable but wise and merciful law of nature.

A　　U　　T

Tender October

October is a flamboyant month with vast sweep of color, blinding in its glory, matchless skies of sapphire blue, sleepy, lazy haze hanging over the hills and creeping slyly down into valleys and out across the field and plain. It is a storehouse of treasure, harvest and opulence.

But October also has its tender moments, homey little touches, silence for contemplation and rest. These precious intimacies never happen with gusto, announced by trumpets and cymbals. Most times they happen unexpectedly out of the busyness of the day and are all the more cherished for that very reason. They come as a quiet benediction but are powerful as "the still small voice."

One gentle episode comes from an unexpected source, the mockingbird. One would not expect a show of sensitivity from a bird known for his bluff and bluster, but it does. The mockingbird is singing now, not to the great wide world but to himself. His voice is soft, low, almost ventriloquial, very musical and subdued.

He sings his own musical composition and if he must help himself to other birds' tunes he's likely to incorporate the soft music of the bluebird, catbird or oriole. But it isn't in the character of the bird to be an inconspicuous, retiring performer. On what stage does he sing? A television aerial or the top of an electric light pole.

One of the very choice unexpecteds is to round a bend in a trail near the little bog at Aullwood Audubon Center and come upon a plant of the exquisite fringed gentian blooming in the sun. What indescribable loveliness in a single flower!

A show of rather unusual, self-protective behavior came from a flock of about 20 English sparrows that call my hilltop home. It was rather prophetic. Just at sundown they scurried about looking for night shelter. Usually they hover under the eaves of my neighbor's barn or my garage, but this evening they sought some natural shelter, the dense foliage of the cork bark euonymous, the taxus, the honeysuckle tangle on the fence. They'd settle, then, dissatisfied, they'd seek another spot that offered good shelter.

The next morning everything was crisp and silvered by our first hard frost. Did the restlessness of the sparrows predict the weather change that brought the frost?

The restlessness was not restricted to the sparrows. A flock of nearly 20 robins scattered over the lawn. Spick and span robins all dolled up in their fine fall plumage. I think robins are handsomer in autumn than in spring. And animated! They made no attempt to eat. They acted as if they were listening to some unseen leader who would momentarily order them onward. A few full of high spirits chased each other across the lawn and then, in a breath, all were gone.

Instincts working deeply within them, the wild creatures indicate a change of behavior, a change of season, a change of time, a change in the way of life.

U   M   N

Winter

God bless all little helpless things:
The lark above that blithely sings,
The new-born lamb in windswept field,
The velvet mole from view concealed,
The rabbit sitting in the hedge,
The robin on my window ledge,
The squirrel with his winter hoard.
All little creatures bless, oh Lord!
God smiles on little things, I'm sure,
He, too, was tiny once, and poor.

Anonymous

Teasel

The teasel, one of our commonest wild plants, is considered a weed, and a formidable one at that. It stands tall and stiff, armored with prickly spines over its entire surface. There is not a single part one can grasp without having the hands painfully punctured, for leaves, stems, flowers and seed heads are armored as effectively as the armor worn by knights of old. Even the tender young leaves of the round rosettes of the first-year growth, prone on the ground, are prickly.

We are apt to look on this prominent stalwart of the plant kingdom with mixed emotions. It is common and abundant. Its appearance is "different" rather than prompting attention. It is repelling rather than appealing, particularly when we come in physical contact with it and its prickly armor.

But the teasel has an ancient and honorable history. If it has fallen on days when it is considered with indifference or with efforts to eradicate it, the fault rests with man rather than with the plant.

Teasels go back a long way. After the Norman invasion of England in 1066, the wool industry flourished. Wool became the source of income for a nation constantly at war on the continent of Europe. Wool paid for the follies and ambitions of kings, mercenary soldiers, government. It built castles, churches, supported monasteries and paid for crusades.

The clothmakers, or drapers, formed the largest and most powerful guild in England. Their insignia was the lamb and the teasel, for the rough, prickly seed head of the teasel was used to raise the nap on woolen cloth. It was vital in putting on the finish of the cloth, bringing out the luster of the color and the guarantee of quality.

It was said that the lamb and teasel might well have carried the coat of arms of London, for this great city on the Thames was founded on wool — and its very necessary attendant teasel.

The teasel is not a native plant in America. It was brought to our shores by colonists of New England, New York and Pennsylvania to raise the nap on all the woolen cloth woven in colonial homes and later in mills. In the mills, teasel seed heads were placed on wheels and the nap was raised by their rotating movement.

Teasel is unique in many ways. How it blooms is one example of its individuality. Some flowers, like the goldenrod start to bloom at the tip of the flowering branches and continue downward to its base. Clovers begin to bloom at the base and work upward. But the teasel begins at the middle and blooms both ways, ringed round with tiny lilac-colored florets. The botanical structure and function of this flower are complicated.

The seed head contains an enormous number of seeds. Once a class at the Dayton Museum of Natural History attempted to count the number of seeds produced by a single flower. It was an impossible task, for the seeds were too tiny to isolate.

Seeds are broadcast by the wind. If all seeds germinated, there certainly would not be room enough for any other species of green plants to grow. Nature is prodigal. There are always teasels, but they are never too abundant and are easily controlled.

Teasel seed heads are handsome. They are a choice addition to an arrangement of dried wayside material. They are lovely bleached white or cream-colored in Clorox. They add much to the interest of the winter landscape as we travel our highways or tramp through wildlife areas, parks and preserves.

Teasel is a weed that throughout the centuries has paid its way. Now it can enjoy its retirement, for sophisticated machinery does the work it did from feudal times in England.

Hoarfrost

Throughout the calendar year, continuing natural phenomena occur that inspire mixed reactions in the human observer. The rainbow spanning the vast expanse of heaven, an eclipse of the sun, the flash of lightning and the crack of thunder, the awesome force of cyclone and blizzard, the blaze of autumn's color, the lofty sweep of the dawn bird chorus strike a response in the human heart and spirit that ranges from joy to terror, serenity to panic.

A phenomenon that brings breathless beauty and a sense of wonderment is the experience of awakening to find the world powdered with hoarfrost.

Hoarfrost appears when two atmospheric conditions are present at the same time — moisture, probably a fog, and a sudden drop in temperature. The veil of fog is turned into microscopic ice crystals that cover trees and shrubs and all the spent vegetation of field and byway with frostiness feather light, silver white, mystic, fey.

Other conditions contribute to the perfection of a land turned to a filigree of ice in its most fragile form. The sky is always gray, hiding a rising sun. It is always windless, for a breath of moving air shatters hoarfrost's frail structure.

The stillness, the unearthly quality of its beauty, the rare shape and form of its ghostly silhouettes, reduce the mundane human to breathless wonder and reverence.

It is all too quickly spent. The sun does shine, and the wind will blow. But before the feeble power of the winter sun melts the frost, it catches every facet of each crystal and turns its silver to shining gold.

The scintillating light sparkles as if millions of diamonds were on display. The effect is startling, blinding. The wind stirs and soon finishes what the sun started. Before our dazzled eyes, the magic disappears and November's dour countenance controls the landscape.

Strangely enough, some winters pass without hoarfrost occurring. During the three successive winters of subnormal cold, hoarfrosts were frequent. Last week there was a spotty display. Here and there a single bush or tree was rimmed with the coating of hoarfrost.

Then we entered a five-mile stretch of country where all vegetation was frosted with the eerie daintiness, the haunting unworldliness of Nature's most exquisite form of enchantment, hoarfrost.

A single crow flapped across the leaden sky and came to roost in a Christmas card tree. His caw reverberated like a round of artillery in the muted quiet of the frosty morning. His black coat gave the contrast needed to perfect the scene.

I hope this will be a hoarfrost winter.

T   E   R

Thanksgiving

Tradition has significance even in the most sophisticated society and the items found on the menu of the first Thanksgiving dinner have first priority as we plan our Thanksgiving feast today.

Friends were invited to share the bounty of harvest on that long gone day dedicated to giving thanks for abundant food, for shelter in a raw, new land, for comparative safety among strangers who had become friends. All these blessings had been hard earned and thanksgiving was, indeed, in order.

Native foods were at hand. Wild turkeys roamed the forest and cranberries clogged the bogs and boggy beds of ancient lakes. Today hardly a Thanksgiving dinner is served without these two traditional foods. The pumpkins for pies and bread probably were grown from seeds brought from England, for the squash and pumpkin we know today were not native to the New World.

The wild turkey is a noble bird. Before our land was settled it roamed the forest from Maine southward and westward. The meat was delicious and the wild turkey was an important food source for both the settler and Indian. They were essentially woodland birds and they became scarce and in some areas disappeared entirely, when the land was cleared for agriculture.

The courtship of the domestic turkey gobbler seen on farms is well known. The wild turkey's display is similar, spreading body feathers and raising the tail feathers into an enormous fan, swelling the naked skin on head and neck and rattling its wing quills.

All the time he is engaged in increasing the size of his body, he struts around like an Indian chief performing a slow dance and gobbles with great gusto.

Turkeys are polygamous and the most convincing gobbler succeeds in attracting the largest number of females to his harem. He recognizes them all. At the end of the egg laying period he is emaciated and exhausted and takes no further interest in the hens. He is not a dedicated parent. In fact, the hens hide their nests, away from his bad temper and jealousy.

The hen seldom leaves her nest while brooding the eggs. Audubon, who had the opportunity of studying the wild turkey as no observer ever will again, watched the hatching of the eggs, the care the hen gave the chicks, helping them out of the shell, caressing them with her bill and grooming them with her beak.

Efforts are made now to establish the wild turkey in Ohio hill country and some progress is reported. It is an expensive operation to raise game birds commercially and release them for hunting. Persons engaged in this business establish their breeding stock from eggs of the wild birds, trapped wild stock and eggs from domestic hens mated to wild gobblers. The success depends on how well the young adapt to living in a wild environment.

Benjamin Franklin stoutly advocated choosing the wild turkey as our national emblem.

W   I   N

Goldfinch

*At some glad moment
    was it Nature's choice
To dower a scrap of
    sunlight with a voice?*

Not only did nature dower the wee, chubby goldfinch with a lyrical voice, light and lilting, but she also gave it a coat of spun gold with definitive touches of black on wings and tail and set a jaunty black cap atop its head. No other bird bounds through the air with such carefree abandon, for it was given the gift of singing in flight.

No wonder that all who see him love him, for he returns our affection with a sunny happiness that brightens the most dismal day. He is a confirmed stay-at-home, for there is little or no migration among goldfinches, so the merry little fellows are found here throughout the year.

Before mating in the spring goldfinches gather in bands, looking like dancing golden butterflies and, singing their canary-like song, they wander all over the countryside. In summer, they feed along fence rows, out into neglected fields and broad lawns where they eat dandelion seeds. They follow flower borders where they feed on the fluffy seed of the coreopsis and cornflower. What prettier picture can you find outdoors than the dainty yellow goldfinch swaying on a spray of blue ragged robin?

Goldfinches behave like the grasshopper in the fable, dancing the summer away with no thought of tomorrow. When late August augurs autumn's approach they regard life as soberly as it is possible for such carefree creatures to manage. They hastily consider family affairs by building snug nests of dried grasses, placing them in the bastion of a prickly bull thistle and lining the nest with thistle down. At the same time the thistle seeds are eaten greedily.

There is a definite affinity between the pretty yellow bird and the stalwart thistle plant with its beautiful lavender flowers and its stiletto-tipped silver-green foliage. Often the goldfinch is called "thistle bird" because of its close association with the plant.

Young goldfinches are perhaps the most appealing of all bird babies. Even in the nest their food calls are musical as if they are saying, "please" and "thank you" as well-mannered children should. Even when they go to the toilet they fastidiously sit on the brim of the nest and drop the egestion over the side.

Late autumn finds the bright gold changed to olive-gray-brown, with only the white on wings showing. This seasonal change confuses many observers who are not aware of the plumage modification.

Goldfinches have made a happy adaptation to changes in their environment. Many years ago they appeared at our urban and suburban gardens where they ate sunflower seeds. Then thistle seed was introduced and the finches' diet was complete. New feeders made of either Plexiglas or mesh were placed on the market. They have small openings to accommodate goldfinches' small beaks, thus eliminating the problem of intruding English sparrows.

So, let me present to you, pure joy, the goldfinch, who will delight you with the warmth of his merry good cheer on cold, bleak days of winter, if you put out his favorite food, thistle and sunflower seeds, in your winter garden.

Busy bird feeder

The feeding area in my winter garden is fluttering with the busyness of goldfinches swooping from feeder to feeder. They alight to rest on terminal twigs of dogwood and hop hornbeam, the pretty designs of white on closed wings showing up sharply against the icebound perches where a few puffs of snow that have not been blown away by the wind still cling.

Below on the hardpacked snow, juncos, song sparrows, a few doves, a single white-throated sparrow and a pair of cardinals eat the seed spill from the mesh goldfinch feeders. Even so there is a lot of waste from this type of feeder and although the goldfinches seem to prefer them to the plexiglass style, it hurts my sense of thrift considering the high cost of seed.

Downy woodpeckers hang on the suet feeders and get a meal from the crumbs the greedy starlings have left. One day a flicker came to the suet and gave the starling that tried to dislodge him a vicious peck with his stout beak, sending the intruder scooting. What a fine, handsome bird the flicker is! He does not come to the food regularly, so when he does visit it is an exciting event.

Amid this busy traffic two tiny chickadees come and go to a spherical plexiglass feeder filled with sunflower seeds. The opening is small so the English sparrows leave it alone. The chickadees are the only birds that take advantage of this special accommodation. One waits while the other takes a seed, flies to the Norway spruce, holds the seed with one foot, sheds the outer covering and eats the kernel. The second chickadee then does

a repeat performance. They are polite to each other and there is never a squabble over the food.

Chickadees are the cunningest little creatures imaginable. They are alert, quick, friendly and appealing in looks and behavior. Their pearl gray plumage is accented by a smart black crown and a black spot on the chin. There is a white patch on each cheek. The breast is off-white with a wash of chestnut along the sides.

This little mite endears itself by its agility, the dash and style of every move. He inspects small branches of trees and shrubs, moving his body with incredible speed and taking impossible positions, standing on his head as often as upright. All the time he gives his merry winter call, chick-a-dee-dee-dee, one of the happiest sounds in the outdoors. As he dashes about he eats all kinds of latent insects, insect egg masses, small cocoons, and destructive scales. His feeding is of great economic value.

This tiny bird, besides being the personification of good cheer, has the heart of a lion. He comes through the cruel cold of winter with great courage. I've seen chickadees fly into the yard with ice on wings and tail, their balance disturbed, flight difficult, yet they waited patiently for the weak winter sun to melt the ice.

Will the use of sprays in our orchards eventually exterminate this source of pleasure and inspiration, this precious bit of animation that flies through its existence ANY side up WITHOUT CARE?

W   I   N

Geese

Many years ago, before farmers used mechanized methods for harvesting their corn, the fields, picturesque with their long precise rows of corn shocks and splashed with color of bright orange pumpkins, presented a picture typical of autumn.

Early in the morning the scene floated in rising mist which the sun soon burned off, leaving the broad fields to bask in its tempered warmth under the clear untroubled blue of the sky.

The farmer, working in the fields on such a day in such a scene, often heard high overhead a sound he anticipated and enjoyed, the stirring honking of wild geese. The sound sifted to earth and looking upward he watched them approach, a long stream of great strong birds with a gallant leader at the front of the V-shaped formation, piloting them south to their wintering grounds.

The honking of the geese, the birds themselves, were part of the bracing weather, the unlimited expanse of sky, the uninhibited freedom of creatures blest with the gift of flight. Their coming was a portent of a change in weather, a shift of seasons.

A feeling of mystery was evoked at the sound of their wild, free cry, wonder at the ordered formation of their converging lines, and respect for the wisdom shown by their guided flight.

Many of the farms are gone, but the birds still pass. Their nesting sites far north still remain and the waterways to the south where they spend the winter still sparkle in the sun.

From the sky the wise old leaders recognize landmarks and places to stop for rest and food. They might sometimes be confused or delayed by fog and blizzards, but the instinctive memory, instilled by generations of experience, leads the flock through peril and obstacles to their destination.

Strength and stability characterize the personality of the Canada goose. It is widely distributed over the continent and is recognized and admired even by the most casual observer.

The Canada goose is large, handsome, intelligent, faithful and capable. And yet he has a dual personality when it comes to his personal safety. He is the most wary and suspicious of all birds on his breeding grounds and when he alights to feed and rest on his migrating journey.

In spite of these traits he is easily tamed and quickly becomes domesticated.

We often see Canada geese at farm ponds where they have chosen to stay. Last year at Stonybrook farm near Waynesville a flock rested for awhile on the lake there. A gander became enamored by a domestic goose and when the wild flock left, he decided to remain.

Canada geese mate for life. It is well known that often when one dies the mate dies of grief and loneliness. Because of his devotion to his mate, the male is a staunch defender of his nest. He is fierce in battling any intruder and will fight to his death if necessary for safety of the nest and brooding female.

T   E   R

A song, a star, a child

There's a song in the air, there's a star in the sky,
There's a mother's deep prayer and a baby's low cry.
And the star rains its fire as the beautiful sing
For the manger of Bethlehem cradles a King.

The song? A multitude of the heavenly host singing the Gloria and "peace on earth to men of good will." The Vulgate interpretation of the song makes good sense. Other translations — "peace on earth, good will toward men" — suggest a gift to be kept or lightly tossed aside.

Peace on earth to men of good will implies a responsibility — that peace can be achieved only by effort, the exercise of good will that is found within every human heart.

A star in the sky! There never was such a star! Astronomers believe it to have been a nova, but it lit a dark cave manger with searing light brighter than any moonglow and led the wondering shepherds and, later, the Magi "to the place where the young child lay."

And so the long-awaited child was born, a birth that was prophesied from the beginning, in Genesis, the Psalms, by the prophets Isaiah and Micah. It was a birth of contrast — heavens aglow by power from a mysterious, never-before-seen sky light, the radiant presence of a shining heavenly choir singing triumphant music and a lowly manger in a stable-cave with bewildered domestic animals looking on at the strange scene, their rest disturbed by events incredible.

In his prophecy of this baby's birth, Isaiah predicted "the government shall be upon his shoulders and his name shall be Wonderful, Counsellor the Mighty God, the Everlasting Father, the Prince of Peace."

It was fitting that the angel of the Lord should announce the birth of this child first to the shepherds out in the hills beyond the little town of Bethlehem, watching their sheep. They were men of simple piety, rugged and weathered from the rough outdoor labor of tending their flocks and keeping them from straying, protecting them from wild animals that preyed in the night. Their livelihood depended on keeping the flock safe; even the weakest newborn lamb was tenderly cared for, for the loss of one sheep or lamb was important to the economy. They regarded lambs as symbols of purity and innocence.

The baby grew in stature, He waxed strong and became a comely, compelling

adult, but He never became a grandiose person who threw His weight about. In his poem, *The Lamb*, the English poet, William Blake, wrote, "He was meek and He was mild,"and like the lamb, in time He was referred to reverently as the Lamb of God.

All His life, He trod the outdoor way. The hills, the mountains were a place to retire, to restore strength of body and spirit, to meditate, to commune with the Father. The Jordan River was the scene of an important event in His life, and the Sea of Galilee meant more than a traffic thoroughfare and center of the fishing industry.

The sunlit, rippling fields with their lush plant life delighted Him, and He used them to emphasize a point in His teaching: "Consider the lilies of the field. They toil not, neither do they spin, yet Solomon in all his glory was not arrayed as one of these." A parable about the mustard seed, a common plant, was easily made clear to the country people to whom He talked.

Even in His day, the sparrow (probably the English sparrow that we know, a member of the oriental family of weaver finches) was everywhere. He used it as an illustration of the Father's unfailing concern for His children; "If He is aware of the sparrow's fall, how much more concerned would He be about the welfare of His human children."

The desert was a place to feed His many guests. In Dublin, in the National Gallery of Ireland, is a magnificent painting of Him feeding 5,000 people. His face glows with pleasure as He walks among the people serving them the humble fare of bread and fish.

He spent the last evening of His life in a Garden, and the next day He died on a cross dug deep on a hill. He never lived up to Isaiah's grand-sounding names, but He was recognized as the Son of God and the Lamb of God who taketh away the sins of the world. In His brief life, He turned the world around and pointed mankind in a new direction.

He had one mission in life: "I am come that ye might have life and have it more abundantly." He gave us a new commandment: ". . . that ye love one another. Thou shalt love thy neighbor as thyself. There is none other commandment greater than this."

The wee babe born in the lowly manger was Christ, the Lord. Like the humble shepherds and the resplendent oriental kings, we celebrate His birthday with joy and thanksgiving, singing, "Gloria in excelsis Deo, peace on earth to men of good will."

T   E   R

Cardinal

Throughout the spring and summer days we enjoy the music of the cardinal.

His song is loud, strong and clear. No nonsense about it, either.

There are no frills and off-shoot tangents about it that might confuse the ear of the uninitiated or the listener who does not have the ability to identify a song quickly and accurately.

When a cardinal sings you know it is a cardinal, not some other bird whose music sounds like that of a cardinal. You have respect for such a decisive musician, and you settle back and enjoy his concerts. There are many accomplished singers among the birds, but, to me, there is nothing more beautiful than the sweet simply whistled tune of the cardinal as he performs in my garden at twilight on a summer evening.

He has several songs to sing. If you know cardinal music at all you can easily recognize them.

In the past, we have had several injured cardinals in the museum. They have been hurt in such a way that they could not care for themselves if they remained at liberty. These birds quickly adapt themselves to captivity, and, much to our pleasure, they sing their full songs, even though they are restricted to a cage.

For a long time now, there have been no cardinals in our animal fair room, so I was surprised when I heard the loud carrying whistle of the cardinal ringing out from that area. Thinking that another cardinal must have been brought in, I investigated, but found no such bird there.

Later on I heard the cardinal singing again, I checked outside to determine if I were hearing a bird singing on our grounds. None was there.

Now I began to suspect that there must be an imitator in the room. I made a quick inventory of the captive birds: screech owl, great horned owl, sparrowhawk, mourning dove, crows and blue jay.

Of them all, the crows were suspect, for they talk, quack like ducks and make a conglomerate of sounds so convincingly, that one would not be surprised if all at once one might have learned to whistle.

By this time the rest of the staff was interested in the mystery. Every time we heard a cardinal we rushed to the animal room to see the bird in the act of singing, but we had no success.

Then one day I heard the lovely song of the cardinal, sweet and clear, and tiptoeing to a window that looks into the room, I peeked in and saw the culprit singing with all his might, pumping his body up and down singing the "pretty girl, pretty girl," song of the cardinal! It was the blue jay!

Of course the next thing to do was to find out if this is a strange occurrence. In looking up many references on bird song, especially in regard to the blue jay's musical efforts, we found that most authorities refer only to his imitating the call of the red shouldered hawk.

Then we struck pay dirt.

In Forbush's *Birds of New England* this excellent bird authority reported having heard the blue jay imitate the song of the Baltimore oriole and the whisper song of the catbird.

But nowhere did we find any record of a blue jay singing the song of the cardinal. So we have a distinguished and accomplished blue jay in the long cylindrical cage in the animal room of the Dayton Museum of Natural History.

W   I   N

Year's end

The last page on the calendar announces the death of the old year. Beneath its dog-eared sheet lies the new calendar from the American Museum of Natural History, 12 pages, each timing a month, neatly dividing the New Year into 366 days, since this is leap year.

In our clock-regulated existence, we need the guide of a calendar. We need a calendar to remind us that December has ended and January is here. A mathematical division of time is necessary, for the weather has been no help at all. The 1979 December, on those days when the sun was visible, seemed more like October, the gray days like March, with its winds pruning the trees and leaving the ground cluttered with its trimming.

Calendar-wise, it is a new year. Yet every year in nature is not timed by mathematical precision. The only measurement that is precise is that our year is divided into seasons, a time for preparation and planting, growing, harvesting and resting.

Seasons often overlap, blending inconspicuously one into another, sometimes shifting duties. Time was when farmers always plowed the land in spring as soon as the soil was dry, a condition often delayed by a prolonged spell of wet weather. Now farmers take advantage of sunny, dry days in autumn to plow their fields, leaving the long, straight furrows exposed to the freezing and thawing of winter, which aerates the soil and makes it friable for spring planting.

The days pass, blending smoothly into each other. So pass the years. There is a continuity of all the years expressed in the forests, grass, the rise and ebb of the tides, the never-failing parade of wildflowers, the faith of the birds on their long migrations, the solidarity of the hills, the mountains' snow-capped majesty and man, even though his present performance of carrying on his species is not too honorable or admirable.

The continuity found in nature is what matters. The resting season ends, and a new year begins. It is the continuity that sustains and brings calm and understanding in the face of natural disaster. It creates hope and trust during periods of a balanced norm. Spring comes when new life emerges from the continuity of the seed, the bulb, the root. The continuity of the egg renews life in the animal world — the spider, the insect, the fish, the frog, the reptile, the bird, the lamb, the child.

The continuity of cause and effect often results in bewilderment to the human mind, for it produces beauty and awe, delight and terror alike in our existence — the rainbow and the hoarfrost, the raindrop and the snowflake, the gentle breeze and the tornado, the snow and the avalanche, rain and flood, volcano and earthquake.

So the year neither begins nor does it end. Its mathematical division into minutes, hours, days and months has been devised by the mind of man for his own convenience. It reminds him when to keep appointments, pay taxes and consider his own advancing age. It is the continuity in nature that counts, and it is not timed by the calendar or clock.

T E R

Kudos to Quinn

Kudos to Bob Quinn! Robert Quinn is a retired mail clerk, a recognized, published poet, a retiring and gentle man, whose paths lead to the outdoors, for he loves "all creatures great and small." He views nature through the poet's eyes, with the poet's appreciation and compassion.

But there's a streak of practicality in Bob's soul, as you shall soon learn. When on a walk near his apartment on Jan. 9, he saw a flock of 14 robins feeding on the fruit of three Washington hawthorne trees. He felt pleased that there seemed to be an ample supply, for these birds are finicky in their choice of food. Because their beaks are soft they feed principally on fruit and berries, soft insects and earthworms. As this kind of food isn't easily found in winter, robins fly south in the fall, where their preferred food is available.

Bob thought the birds would move on when the food was depleted, but they didn't. Temperatures were dropping and snow deepened each day and the robins lingered.

Only one thing to do, thought Bob, and he did it. He chopped up some apples he had on hand, found some raisins in his cupboard, bought some suet, crumbled it into tiny pieces, shoved it into a shopping bag and scattered it on the ground under the haw trees behind the United Methodist Church building at Riverside and Grafton Avenue, and an apartment house farther up the street on Grafton.

The robins found the food immediately. The weather worsened, deep snow, now, and below zero temperatures prevailed. Bob, now bundled up like someone headed for an Arctic exploration, trudged through the snow and, battered by the bitter wind, distributed food twice daily to the robins. They anticipated his visits. A male, evidently a scout, spied him from the topmost twig of the tree and chirped excitedly at his approach.

Soon Bob was baking cornbread for his pensioners. The cornbread, rich in shortening, provided fat which helps maintain a high rate of metabolism. It also softened the crumbs, which helps robins to swallow the nutritious food without scratching their throats. He learned that they also like macaroni and cheese, which, added to the fruit diet, kept the birds in fine fettle.

Robert Quinn doesn't have an Irish name for nothing. His sense of humor bubbles

W   I   N

over into chuckles when he visualizes the picture he must present to people he passes as he wades through the snow en route to his bird feeding chores.

An old fur cap is held firm to his head against the tug of the wind by two woolen scarves that cover his ears and wind around his neck. A heavy coat and pant legs stuffed into high boots show how the well-dressed man should look when he ventures out in the ghastly weather to feed 14 robins.

He starts out with a snow shovel under one arm and he carries a shopping bag and a small red suitcase filled with food in either hand. He thinks the scout recognizes the red suitcase and starts up a lively chirping to gather the clan when he sees Bob coming.

On his way to the feeding trees Bob often passes an elderly gentleman walking two small house dogs. The man gives Bob a queer look when they meet and Bob felt he owed an explanation of his strange getup to the man, who eyed him suspiciously.

"Good morning," Bob greeted him one morning.

A grunt served as a reply.

"I'm out to feed the robins up the street," Bob explained, thrusting the food bags forward as evidence.

"Robins all gone south," the man informed Bob.

"But sometimes some stay and these need food now."

"Starlings. You're just feeding starlings."

"No, sir," Bob insisted. "These birds have russet breasts and black heads."

The man shoved past Bob and walked on. Bob heard him say to the dogs, "Fool's feeding starlings," and gave a cackling laugh. Bob swears the dogs laughed right back at the man, all three laughing at the absurdity of feeding starlings!

Bob was convulsed with laughter. He, too, laughed so hard the tears rolled down and froze on his face.

Bob Quinn spent the last 16 winters in Florida and intended to go there this winter. But he knew he couldn't be warm and comfortable in Florida knowing a small flock of robins depended on him to see them through one of the roughest winters ever experienced in Ohio. So he stayed in Dayton. He suffers arthritic pains and has had a cold but his compassion has overcome any physical discomfort he feels and he sees that 14 robins get two good meals a day.

God rest ye, merry Bob Quinn!

T   E   R

January light

January's light on a cloudless day has a unique air of distinction unlike that of any other month in the year. It does not persist throughout the entire day — only in early morning hours and again in late afternoon just before the sun drops below the horizon.

It is a heady clearness like the quality of brilliance seen in fine crystal. The light seems brittle. One has the feeling that, if it could be held in the hands, it could easily be broken.

This strange quality of light was demonstrated lately on a clear, cold morning as I looked at the long drooping twigs on a weeping willow tree. The scintillating light caught and radiated the tawny grace of the twigs against the background of the special hue of mid-winter blue sky. It seemed that the play of light centered entirely on the willow tree.

In snow drifts sculpted by the wind into sharp angles and wind-blasted hollows, January light causes a play of light and shadow that casts a coloring of blue, very dark blue and purple. This is a rare type of beauty dependent largely upon the light.

Perhaps this electrifying structure of light that is peculiar to this time of year results from the winter solstice, when the great sun starts its journey north, bringing light to the dark forests and fertility to the fields, the streams and the flocks. The vibrant light stimulates; it holds the subtle promise of spring, even when the world is in the throes of winter.

It is the time when the song sparrow sings its first pre-nuptial song, a vocalizing effort to clear its throat of winter's huskiness. Crows' caws are high-pitched and excited, the titmouse's whistle spirited. Little streams start humming under their ceiling of ice.

Everywhere there are abundant signs of rabbits. Their tracks in the snow tell where they are or have been. Rabbits had a most successful breeding season last summer, yet the hunter in our family returns empty-handed from every hunting trip.

Each January day is longer than the last. The difference from day to day is slight. Even though January brings bleak weather with deep cold, storm and piling snow, its daylight hours increase, never diminish. Toward the last days of January, daylight will have gained 45 minutes since the first of the month.

January is named for the Roman god Janus. He is depicted with two faces looking in opposite directions: one contemplative, reliving the past; the other prospective, looking forward expectantly to the future with hope and promise.

W   I   N

Snow

A sharp wind rattles the branches of deciduous trees and sends a moan and a sigh through the green depths of the spruce trees. It is a good day to stay indoors, for the wind bites and stings.

Even birds have holed in. Every window in the house frames a picture of the snowbound land, covered by a deep, white blanket. It is a strange paradox that snow, so cold, also gives warmth, for it is a marvelous insulator. The snow, plus the protection of prostrate junipers on a slope in my neighbor's garden, makes a warm winter covering for the local rabbit population. Tracks running in all directions lead to this snug shelter.

Ground-roosting birds, like the bobwhite and pheasant, keep comfortable when their grass-weed hummocks are arched-over with snow. Piled-up, discarded Christmas trees and branches pruned from yards and orchards make excellent winter cover for wildlife. And, when snow filters through, warmth and safety for birds and small mammals are improved.

The earth itself is improved by snow. Snow prevents winter crops, like wheat, from heaving above ground during normal freezing and thawing of winter. And, when it melts, it releases valuable minerals into the soil.

But how few regard snow as a blessing or see it through the eyes of a delighted child or of those who have grown older without losing the child's sense of wonder, the excitement that the first snowfall brings.

For the soft, clinging, beautiful snow causes inconvenience and hardship. It ties up traffic, interferes with the transaction of the world's business and reduces man's pride and joy, the automobile, to an inefficient hunk of metal. When snow is accompanied by freezing rain, electrical outages occur, and a blizzard puts a halt to everything. Just clearing a path in snow can be a pain in the neck and back.

But who can be insensitive to the beauty of snow? Each flake is an exquisite, hexagonal crystal, lovely in design and texture. It covers our earth, hiding the ugly scars man has made on its surface. It gives the receiving earth, for a time at least, the appearance of innocence and purity.

Snow proves to be an adaptable medium for winds to mold at their will. It cuts chasms and erects peaks. It builds to a depth that obliterates highways and then, for contrast, sweeps some surfaces clean and bare. Light casts fantastic shadows on snow and colors them different shades of blue and green and purple. Varying degrees of cold temperatures play games with snow, or ice crystals, and turn the world into a lacy wonderland of hoarfrost.

Snow is fun. It is fun to walk in snowshoes, to feel the soft cold of it on the face, to have bundled-up clothing covered quickly with its whiteness, to feel deep within the magic, the wonder of it falling silently from the gray sky. Suddenly we feel drawn to the very heart of nature, a participant in its cosmic force.

Snow has a way of recalling past snow fun — making snowmen, going coasting, playing fox and geese in the country school playground and having snowball fights on the way home from school. It also brings to mind a memory gem from Lucia May Wiant's collection.

The snowflakes fall from the soft gray sky
And cover the earth with a mantle fair.
Each tiny flake is a star-shaped pearl
From the mystical, sea-like depths of air.

T E R

Larks

*For Sam Archambeault, friend
and outdoor companion*

"Hark, hark, the lark at heaven's gate sings," wrote Shakespeare in one of his lighter creative moments and Shelley saluted the lark as a "blithe spirit." Of course, both poets were paying tribute to the English skylark, a shy, nondescript bird of the fields whose only claim to adulation is its accomplishment as a songster.

In our country the only true lark is the horned lark, a relative of the European skylark. They are widely distributed over the northern hemisphere and nest in flat areas in all environments except forests. They are seen in our area more frequently in winter than at any other time of the year.

Horned larks endear themselves to bird watchers and they've always been high on my list of favorites. But they are doubly dear to me for the great pleasure they gave to two of my closest bird-watching friends, Sam and Margaret Archambeault. Last week Sam died, leaving his many friends who treasured his warm companionship on field trips and Audubon activities bereft.

During winter's snowbound weather we three frequently drove to the flat country north of Dayton and spent the entire day following the flocks of horned larks that are so numerous in that part of Ohio.

Here no fences enclose the land, no ditches border the roads, only vast, unobstructed stretches of fields extend to the horizon. They are intersected by country roads. Sam would stop the car and we waited. Soon a flock of horned larks would fly low over the ground, settle close by and start feeding. They never ran or hopped, but walked, rapidly and bent slightly forward. Some alighted on the gravel shoulder of the road and fed, wind-scattered weed seeds and tiny bits of digestion-aiding gravel making up the unvaried menu.

Unafraid, they came close to the car and we noted, without the aid of binoculars, the sparrow-like streaked back and wings, light underparts tinted a faint yellow, throats yellow with a broad band of black across the chest. Tail feathers showed black when expanded in flight. Their beauty, however, centered around the startling black and white pattern on the cheeks and the saucy crest of feathers or "horns" above the eyes, a feature that gives the bird its name.

The three of us delighted in the friendliness of these birds, their unique beauty, their graceful undulating flight, their tinkling call, like the breaking of icicles that came clear across the snow-blown fields. Such days were special. The brisk cold, the pristine beauty of the flat land, the intimate closeness of the horned larks, the fun of being together as friends with the same interests, bound closely in affection, will always crowd the memory with happiness and gratitude.

Horned larks seldom come into the confines of an enclosed garden, but the past week a flock of over 50 visited the garden of friends who live beside a large field. With this flock were five snow buntings (rare) and a single Lapland longspur.

The male horned lark shows his true lark qualities when he courts his mate. He rises from a clod or low stone, flies high in the air, singing "and singing still doth soar, and soaring, ever singeth." It is a lilting, tinkling song, pleasing, but in no way comparable to the much lauded music of his cousin, the skylark. At the end of his flight he folds his wings and drops to the earth, landing in the very spot from which he ascended.

So soars the spirit of man when life's pilgrimage ends.

W   I   N

Squeak, the groundhog

It is not often that Groundhog Day falls on the day this column is published. So, to take advantage of the calendar, I want to pay tribute to the memory of a groundhog that brought me great pleasure, for I knew him intimately for a long time and had a deep affection for him.

His name was Squeak. He was a spoiled resident and ruled the roost at the Dayton Museum of Natural History when it was located in downtown Dayton across from the public library.

Squeak occupied a commodious cage in the Animal Room, but because he was tame and friendly, he was given the freedom of the upper floor of the museum and could wander around at will unless the place was crowded with visitors. We could not run the risk of people being thrown into a panic on meeting an "escaped" wild animal. Then, too, it wasn't good for Squeak to become excited by receiving too much attention from people who did not know how to handle him. When such situations developed he was caged.

Squeak was probably the handsomest groundhog ever seen in or out of captivity. He was large. His coarse, gray hair tipped with reddish brown shone with good health and frequent grooming. His eyes were bright and alert and, to those who knew him well, always looked as if he were contemplating some mischief. His small ears were perfect, beautifully shaped and grew neatly close to his head. When Squeak sat erect he assumed the stance all groundhogs take, sitting on his haunches, which, with the aid of his short, brushy tail, made a stout tripod to balance his body.

He knew everybody on the staff and abundantly returned all the kindness and affection they showered upon him. He recognized his name and came when he was called. He liked to be petted, enjoyed being rubbed behind his ears and being fed by hand. He had the habit of stretching up on his hind feet and clinging against his friends by his front toes, plainly begging to be petted.

Often he'd slip away from me when I bent over to pet him and in taking his leave, he'd run his sharp toenails down my shins, making wide gapping runs in my hose. After this happened a time or two, I pretended to ignore his pleas for attention for it became quite costly to replace my damaged hose.

But Squeak chased after me as I tried to avoid him and it became a wild game as to which one of us would reach the safety of my office first. Sometimes he'd be at my heels as we ran into the office and then I'd climb on a chair to escape him. He "treed" me in the chair until someone on the staff heard my cries for help, came to my rescue, caught and caged Squeak until he settled down after all the excitement.

On "his" day photographers from the paper took his picture. Squeak really was a ham actor and posed as if he were an obliging VIP. He was loved by everyone who visited the museum and hundreds of children who participated in our natural history educational program adored him.

In our move to the new museum Squeak caught a cold that developed into pneumonia which caused his death. His stuffed remains in the mammal exhibit at the museum are a poor reminder of the animate Squeak — mischievous, vivacious, fun loving — who brought pleasure to many people.

T　　　　E　　　　R

Snowy owl

One of the most exciting events of winter birdlife in the Miami Valley is the appearance of the snowy owl, a huge bird with a large, rounded head. Its wings are long, broad and slightly rounded, and its feet are large on rather short legs. Both legs and toes are covered with thick feathers that protect the bird from cold. Its fierce eyes are golden yellow. The male is snow white with flecks of black in the plumage. The female is larger than the male and darker.

The snowy owl is circumpolar in the Arctic region and found in both hemispheres. Its numbers and distribution over this immense area are governed by abundance or scarcity of the food supply. Its chief food is the lemming, a small rodent. The lemming population periodically zooms, and, when this occurs, we find a corresponding increase in the population of the snowy owl.

This large owl lives on the tundras of the far north, beyond the limit of trees. It perches on hillocks and large boulders, which gives it favorable position to spot its prey — lemmings, Arctic hares, nesting ducks, etc. The snowy owl is a heavy feeder and examination of the body shows a thick layer of fat under its skin.

Its nest, a shallow depression that the bird scoops out with its feet and lightly lines with moss and lichens, is found on these hillocks. It is believed that the bird could not exist if there were no hillocks on the vast snow plains of the north. In areas where the snowy owl might nest on a cliff or rocky ledge, the eggs are laid on the bare surface with a meager tufting of moss or lichens to prevent them from rolling away.

Naturalists who have studied this owl in its native environment have given us a lively picture of its courtship, which is largely vocal. It makes a "hoot" that is a deep "boom," and the sound carries far in the wild desolation of the tundra. One observer crawled on his stomach some distance to approach a performing bird.

"The owl lifted his head, swelled out his throat enormously, elevated his tail comically until it struck straight up and gave four long, low hoots, bowing violently after each hoot. He then dropped his tail, pranced about awkwardly with toes widely spread as if surveying his surroundings for his mate, and then hooted again."

The nesting habits of the snowy owl are unique, probably developed to fit the physical environment and severe weather conditions in which it exists. The eggs are laid on an irregular schedule; several days may pass before the second egg is laid. Since anywhere from three to eight eggs are laid, the first bird hatched is nearly old enough to be on its own before the last egg is hatched.

This is probably a wise plan of nature, for both old birds must work tirelessly to find enough food for their young, as they require a great amount of food, and consequently they are away from the nest for long periods of time. The oldest young bird keeps the incubating eggs and young birds warm. Even so, infant mortality in this species runs high.

Lemmings control their overpopulation by migrating south and snowy owls follow them down through the Canadian provinces and the northern tier of states in our own country. This southern movement occurs in cycles of five to seven years.

This huge owl is one of our most impressive birds of prey, and to have it wander into our community, so different from the wild desolation of its Arctic home, always is an exhilarating experience for local bird watchers.

W   I   N

'At heaven's gate'

Two chickadees flew to the white pine, gay as a summer breeze. They alighted unerringly on the feeder. Each selected a plump sunflower seed and holding it daintily with tiny feet, skillfully stripped the outer skin and ate the tasty inside with great gusto.

With a graceful sweep of wings upward, they alighted on the swinging suet stick and fed on this warmth-giving food, all the time chortling and "chick-a-deeing" as if they had much to discuss.

They bent over, head down as if measuring the distance between the stick and the ground. More animated, speculative talk followed. Were they saying? — "But she can never reach the suet stick to fill it with fresh food. Her arms are too short."

"The man was so tall and his arms were long and strong. He filled the feeders in no time at all."

"I'm sure the lady will find a way," said one confidently, and off they flew.

A brilliant male cardinal settled himself deliberately on the bright orange ear of field corn just outside the window where he could look inside without his view obstructed by a curtain.

The man, who seldom objected to the way things were run inside his house, was adamant against curtains that interfered with his watching the birds at the feeder.

The cardinal once heard him say that it was an ideal place for the redbird's cousin, the evening grosbeak, to drop in for a visit some winter when it came East. Ever since then the cardinal had an eye out for this strange relative he had never seen.

The cardinal peeked in the window. The man's chair was empty.

Out in the thicket where the man and the lady had planted the hornbeam and dogwood that shaded his beloved bloodroot, twinleaf, mertensia, wild hyacinth, violets and many other wildlings that burst into delicate bloom long before the trees put forth their leaves, a wee chipmunk blinked at the weak winter sun from the opening of the burrow he had built beneath a fossil-encrusted rock.

At length he ventured forth for a little exercise in the warm air of this mild winter day. Strange how quiet it was all about, no stir in the house, no one walking about doing chores in the garden, no one standing quietly, head lifted to catch sight of a bird flying across the sky or to listen to its song or call. Forlornly the little chipmunk returned to the warm coziness of its burrow.

It turned cold during the night and the temperature dropped. The night was long, the distant stars looking down cold, remote on the sleeping earth. At last the morning light broke. The lady went to the window toward the East where she had often stood with the man to see what kind of weather the day would bring and watch the sun rise out of the blaze of color that washed the far horizon.

Never had the sunrise been so vibrant, never had the pink glowed more vividly before the coming of the sun, nor turned to more exquisite shell-rose as it blended upward into the mauve and green and blue expanse of the heavens. This day was ushered in with a special kind of glory, for on this day, the great loving spirit of the man went to glory, too.

T   E   R

Index

114

Author

Edith Blincoe was born on Shakespeare's birthday in Peebles, Ohio, in Adams County's beautiful hill country. When she was an infant her family moved to Columbus and later they lived in a rural community of broad fields and scattered woodlands. As a child she loved the fields and learned the names of the birds and flowers found there.

Her family moved to Dayton when she was ready for high school and she attended Steele High School. She has lived in Dayton ever since. She was graduated from Teacher's College at Miami University at Oxford.

She pays tribute to her teachers on every educational level saying they were dedicated and capable. She especially recalls the inspiration and personal example set by teachers at Steele.

Her first teaching position at Knoop Children's Home in Miami County lasted four years. She then taught four years in a Dayton elementary school. A year of special training at Miami University in the teaching of retarded children was followed by her working in that field for four years.

Then she met Ben Blincoe and her life took a new direction. He and his two brothers operated a greenhouse and nursery, but he was fundamentally a naturalist, a gentle man with the ability to transmit his love and understanding of nature to others. Ultimately they were married and of him, she says, "I could not have had a more competent mentor or compatible outdoor companion. Ben did more than share my love for the outdoors, he refined and polished it."

For sixteen years until her retirement in 1966 she was on the staff of the Dayton Museum of Natural History as director of children's work.

In 1942 she began her weekly column in *The Journal Herald.* This book was compiled from those weekly columns.